WARRIOR • 127

# NATIVE AMERICAN CODE TALKER IN WORLD WAR II

**ED GILBERT**                    ILLUSTRATED BY RAFFAELE RUGGERI

First published in Great Britain in 2008 by Osprey Publishing,
Midland House, West Way, Botley, Oxford OX2 0PH, United Kingdom
443 Park Avenue South, New York, NY 10016, USA
Email: info@ospreypublishing.com

A CIP catalogue record for this book is available from the British Library.

ISBN 978 1 84603 269 1

Page layout by Mark Holt
Index by Alison Worthington
Typeset in Sabon and Myriad Pro
Originated by PDQ Digital Media Solutions
Printed and bound in China through Worldprint Ltd.

08 09 10 11 12    10 9 8 7 6 5 4 3 2 1

FOR A CATALOGUE OF ALL BOOKS PUBLISHED BY OSPREY MILITARY
AND AVIATION PLEASE CONTACT:

NORTH AMERICA
Osprey Direct, c/o Random House Distribution Center, 400 Hahn Road,
Westminster, MD 21157
Email: info@ospreydirect.com

ALL OTHER REGIONS
Osprey Direct UK, PO Box 140, Wellingborough,
Northants, NN8 2FA, UK
Email: info@ospreydirect.co.uk

Osprey Publishing is supporting the Woodland Trust, the UK's leading
woodland conservation charity, by funding the dedication of trees.

**www.ospreypublishing.com**

## ARTIST'S NOTE

Readers may care to note that the original paintings from which the color
plates in this book were prepared are available for private sale.
All reproduction copyright whatsoever is retained by the Publishers.
All inquiries should be addressed to:

Raffaele Ruggeri
Via Indipenza 22
Bologna 40121
Italy

The Publishers regret that they can enter into no
correspondence upon this matter.

## AUTHOR'S DEDICATION AND ACKNOWLEDGMENTS

For the code talkers of all tribes, who served and died in dutiful anonymity.

I would like to thank the staff of the Marine Corps Heritage Center, Regan
Grau of the Museum of The Pacific War (Fredericksburg, Texas), and Karen
Carver and the staff of The Marriott Library at The University of Utah,
Salt Lake City.

The research of William C. Meadows and Judy Allen has identified the
Choctaw and Comanche code talkers who served with the US Army in
the 36th Division (World War I) and the 4th Infantry Division (World War II).
Nolly Bird is a wholly fictional character whom I have inserted into the
small original band of Comanche recruits. The Marine Corps code talker
program was so deeply shrouded in secrecy that the total number of code
talkers who served is unknown, and many died without even their families
knowing the nature of their service. The characters Winston Chee, Billy
Chee, and Vernon Begay are wholly fictional. The specific experiences
of the fictional characters are not intended to represent the actual
experiences of any one person, though they are based in fact.
All photographs are from the National Archives or the author's collection.

## EDITOR'S NOTE

For ease of comparison between types, imperial measurements are used
almost exclusively throughout this book. The exception is weapon calibers,
which are given in their official designation, whether metric or imperial. The
following data will help in converting the imperial measurements to metric:

1 mile = 1.6km
1lb = 0.45kg
1 yard = 0.9m
1ft = 0.3m
1in. = 2.54cm/25.4mm
1 gal = 4.5 liters
1 ton (US) = 0.9 tonnes
1hp = 0.745kW

# CONTENTS

# NATIVE AMERICAN CODE TALKER IN WORLD WAR II

## INTRODUCTION

Security of communications has been a primary concern of military commanders since prehistoric times. Tactical communications security is particularly problematical, since messages must be sent and received as rapidly as possible under great stress. Considerable intellectual effort has also been expended in code-breaking, as knowledge of the enemy's intentions is one of the greatest advantages a commander can possess.

In 1941 the United States already possessed virtually unbreakable codes thanks to the use of indigenous language. The indigenous peoples of the Americas were divided into local tribes speaking hundreds of languages. Only a few had ever been written, in long-forgotten pictographic alphabets. As the United States expanded westward, the government sought to "civilize the savages." Native languages were to be eradicated. The young were often harshly punished for using their Native languages, and it was hoped that the languages would die out with the older generations.

Early radios were not a practical means of battlefield communication. This radio party in 1918 is trying to establish contact. The long bamboo poles were dragged along to support the wire antenna. (NARA)

But in 1918 the US Army discovered, quite by accident, that Native languages had immense military value. Easily spoken by a Native speaker, they were hard to learn because of the vocabularies and numerous dialects, and had fundamentally different linguistic structures.

The first code talkers were Choctaws from Oklahoma serving in the 142nd Regiment, 36th Division on the Western Front in World War I. The Army had a policy of full integration of Native American troops, but units of the 36th Division were recruited from the old Indian Territory (Oklahoma), and included both Native American and white troops.

The first use of Choctaw in October 1918 was incidental, and simply involved James Edwards and Solomon Lewis speaking their most familiar language to relay information. Radios of the era were heavy and fragile, and saw little practical use in tactical communications. Most communications were by prearranged color-coded rockets, small notes carried by pigeons, electronic buzzers, runners, and field telephones in order of increasing usefulness. Runners were used to coordinate actions of front-line units, but about one in four was

Code talker privates first class Preston and Frank Toledo in Australia, July 1943. The radio is a TBX-7, used in the artillery net. There were several models of the TBX, differentiated by frequencies and tactical application. (NARA)

Field telephones provided reliable front-line communications, but the process of laying and maintaining networks of lines was slow and dangerous. This German wire party illustrates the large entourage necessary to lay a line. (NARA)

killed or captured. Telephones were by far the most satisfactory, but posed serious problems of laying networks of ground lines under fire, and security. Both sides tended to tap into existing wire networks in captured ground, using the enemy's lines. The Germans could easily listen in. This was made obvious by an incident when the Americans discussed the location of a bogus supply point, and the Germans obligingly bombarded the empty ground.

Though senior officers were credited with the idea, the Choctaw code talkers recognized a company commander, one Capt Lawrence, a white officer, as the author of the notion of a formal spoken code. He persuaded senior officers to redistribute eight fluent Choctaw speakers through the battalion. Choctaw communicators eventually served in three regiments, and an unknown number of other tribal language speakers (Cherokee, Cheyenne, Comanche, Osage, and Yankton) were used. Since many military terms – like artillery – had no Choctaw equivalent, simple substitutions like "big gun" were devised. The communicators thwarted every German attempt to break this "code," and taunted eavesdroppers in English and German.

But the successes of the code talkers were largely forgotten. The US Army again experimented with spoken codes as early as 1941, but it fell to the Marine Corps to develop the most comprehensive and secure system of code talking. However, America's potential enemies had not forgotten the code. John Benally said that as a Navajo high-school student in 1936 he assisted an older European man, probably a German, to compile a Navajo vocabulary.

There has been some controversy and acrimony over who originated the idea of the Navajo code. Benally, one of the "Original 29" code talkers, made it clear that Philip Johnston originated the idea, but played no role in development of the code itself. Johnston, the son of missionaries, had grown up on the Navajo reservation. In February 1942 he proposed to Maj James E. Jones the idea of *Dineh* (the name the Navajo call themselves) communicators. His idea was to develop a complex code based on the language. This was the birth of true code talking, an unbreakable code within a code.

 **A**  **CHOCTAW CODE TALKER, 142ND INFANTRY, 36TH (INFANTRY) DIVISION, US ARMY IN THE MEUSE-ARGONNE OFFENSIVE, 1918**

The senior leadership of the US Army was determined to break out of the trench warfare stalemate that had characterized the Western Front for four years, and restore mobility to the battlefield. The Meuse-Argonne offensive succeeded in rupturing the German Front, but as in earlier phases of the war communications and logistics limited the advance of any victorious army. In particular, laying secure telephone lines under fire was a slow and hazardous task. This code talker has tapped into an existing German field telephone network by simply splicing his portable telephone into the wires. Many Germans spoke fluent English, and the use of an obscure language like Choctaw thwarted German efforts to eavesdrop on the American communications. The code talker and the infantryman providing security wear the bulky and heavy woolen greatcoat, "dishpan" helmet, and wrap leggings. Both men wear gas-mask carriers around their necks. The communicator is talking on the telephone headset, and the optional headphones are clipped around the telephone box for convenience. Metal tobacco tins, like the one to the right of the telephone, were often used to store parts that might be damaged by water or dirt. The trench knife with integral brass knuckles was a multi-purpose tool, used both for fighting and for cutting and splicing wires.

**Marine division assault communications (typical)**

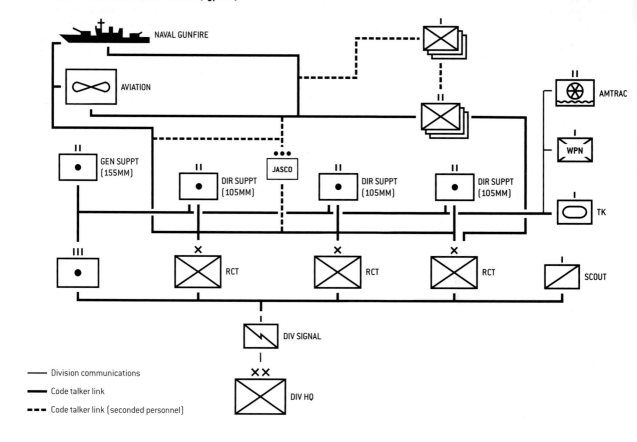

NAVAL GUNFIRE

AVIATION

AMTRAC

WPN

TK

GEN SUPPT
(155MM)

JASCO

DIR SUPPT
(105MM)

DIR SUPPT
(105MM)

DIR SUPPT
(105MM)

RCT

RCT

RCT

SCOUT

DIV SIGNAL

DIV HQ

—— Division communications

━━ Code talker link

■■■ Code talker link (seconded personnel)

Heavy wire reels like this one were used to lay the main telephone lines that knitted together front-line infantry and artillery positions. Maneuvering this burden across the battlefield was a dangerous task. (NARA)

Whichever individuals can best be credited for the adoption of code talkers, they became an integral part of every Marine division, as well as special units like Amphibious Corps support units and Raider units. Some divisions used the code talkers extensively, while others were not so accepting of the program. Some units saw such value in the code that they requested additional code talkers over and above the number rated, or simply grabbed up additional code talkers outside the normal personnel replacement channels. Because of the secrecy that cloaked the program there are no accurate records of how many code talkers served in various units. The diagram above provides some indication of the numbers of code talkers rated by various units, but should not be considered definitive.

This book will cover the development of the code and follow its use and speakers into combat. In addition, it will touch upon the experiences of the much smaller group of Comanche code talkers who served with the US Army in Europe. It should be noted that Comanche code talkers also served in the Pacific War, and Meskwaki, Sioux, Crow, Hopi, and Cree code talkers served with the Army in North Africa and Europe. Little is known about their service.

We will follow four fictional characters, Navajos Winston Chee, Billy Chee, Vern Begay, and Comanche Nolly Bird. All named characters other than these four are actual persons. Where statements from actual persons are enclosed in quotation marks, these indicate quotations extracted from interviews conducted as part of the Marine Corps Historical Division Oral History Program.

Most Army and Marine Corps communicators, like these Marines on Bougainville, used a small mechanical typewriter, which converted each letter of a message into number groups that had to be laboriously transmitted, and decoded at the other end. The process could take several hours, and the message might contain many errors. (NARA)

# CHRONOLOGY

## 1918

**October 26**     The Choctaw language is used to coordinate the withdrawal of two companies of the 142nd Infantry, 36th Division from an exposed position. Additional use of code talkers follows.

## 1940

**December 1940 – January 1941**     (dates uncertain) First Comanche are recruited for the Army's code talker program.

## 1941

**August 1–17**     First code talkers are employed in the Army's Louisiana Maneuvers.

**September–October**     The Comanche code is developed at Camp Benning, Georgia. The system is not destined to be expanded beyond one company.

**December 1941 – January 1942**     (exact date unknown) Philip Johnston contacts Maj James E. Jones, US Marine Corps, with a proposal for a Navajo code.

## 1942

**February 28**     At Camp Elliott, Philip Johnston and four Navajo provide a practical demonstration for Jones, MajGen Clayton B. Vogel, and staff.

**March 26**     LtCol Wethered Woodworth, after meeting with Bureau of Indian Affairs (BIA) officials, recommends recruiting Navajo as code talkers.

**April**     1st Sgt Frank Shinn begins recruiting efforts at Fort Defiance, Arizona.

| | |
|---|---|
| **May 4** | First class of Navajo is inducted at Fort Wingate, Arizona; they are bussed to California the following day. |
| **June 27** | First class of Navajo recruits graduates boot camp. |
| **June 28 – August 23** | First class trains in basic communications and develops the code. |
| **September 18** | First contingent of code talkers arrives on Guadalcanal. Not even the commanding general on the island is aware of the highly secret code program, and at first no one knows how best to utilize the code talkers. The code talkers will go on to play a vital but virtually unknown role in every Marine Corps operation for the next three years. |

## 1943

| | |
|---|---|
| **November** | 6th Marines Division lands on Tarawa. |

## 1944

| | |
|---|---|
| **February** | 4th Marines Division lands on Roi-Namur. |
| **July 15** | 6th Marines Division lands on Saipan. |

## 1945

| | |
|---|---|
| **February–March** | Operation *Detachment*, the assault on Iwo Jima. |
| **March–June** | Operation *Iceberg*, the invasion of Okinawa. |
| **June 19** | On southern Okinawa LtGen Mitsuri Ushijima sends a farewell message to Japan and commits ritual suicide. The ground war is concluded. |
| **August 14** | Japan surrenders unconditionally. |

## 1968

| | |
|---|---|
| **Summer** | Lee Cannon, a member of the Honors Committee of the 4th Division Association, plans to honor the code talkers at the Association's annual reunion. He does not know the code is still classified. |

In addition to man-portable radios, code talkers also manned communications jeeps like this one on Peleliu. (NARA)

## 1969

**June 28**    With the Navajo Code officially declassified by the Marine Corps, the surviving code talkers are honored at the annual reunion in Chicago.

## 1982

**August 14**    The first National Navajo Code Talkers' Day is celebrated on the orders of President Reagan.

## 2000

**December 21**    President Clinton signs a congressional bill to award the Congressional Gold Medal to the original 29 code talkers, and Silver Medals to some 300 Navajo who subsequently served in the program.

## 2001

**July 26**    President Bush awards the medals at a ceremony in the Capitol Rotunda.

## 2002

**June 11**    The film "Windtalkers," an overly dramatized and entirely fictional cinematic version of the code talker story, premiers in Los Angeles.

# ENLISTMENT

Recruitment of the original group of code talkers was by word of mouth, though the purpose was shrouded in secrecy. Navajo John Benally recalled: "I was working for the Bureau of Indian Affairs (BIA) at that time, the education department and the announcement was made that they needed some Navajos to go into special training. I didn't know exactly what the special training was, but of course later on when we were recruited, we were notified of this special program." Carl Gorman was working for the federal government, taking an inventory of Navajo tribal livestock. Upon the outbreak of war the program was suspended, and Gorman lost his job. With few other jobs available on the reservation, the military seemed a good alternative to unemployment.

Winston Chee was working for the Tribal Council when the Indian Placement Bureau in far away Los Angeles, California, contacted him. After an interview with a serious middle-aged man named Philip Johnston, Winston was asked to travel to a place north of San Diego. Johnston explained that his only task would be to stand ready in case any of four other Navajo were taken sick or injured. On February 28, 1942, Winston simply cooled his heels while Johnston and Maj Jones had one of the men translate a message and send it by telephone to another Navajo. The second man translated the message back into English. MajGen Clayton B. Vogel, commander of Amphibious Forces, Pacific Fleet, was impressed by the speed and accuracy of the translation. The Marines were still using an obsolete numerical code called Shackle. Vogel forwarded a report to Washington, and requested permission to recruit 200 Navajo communicators.

Commandant Thomas Holcomb approved only a pilot program of 30 recruits. Influential persons in the military and BIA expressed serious doubts. If the first group of recruits failed, Holcomb could easily end the program.

The Marines set up recruiting posts near the Tribal Headquarters at Fort Defiance, New Mexico, and the two boarding schools. The requirements were that recruits should fall in the age range 18–30 years, have fluency in English

U. S. MARINE CORPS MESSAGE

| TIME FILED | | MSG CEN No. | | HOW SENT |
|---|---|---|---|---|
| (PRECEDENCE) | (SUBMIT TO MESSAGE CENTER IN DUPLICATE) | | | (CLASSIFICATION IF OTHER THAN (CONFIDENTIAL) |

No. _____ 6 _____ DATE _____ 8 JUNE 1944

ACTION To _____ INFO. To _____

MSG #2 TO BN
SIGNS LARGE BODY TROOPS
CROSSED STREAM VICINITY MAP
OVERLAY 2 X PROCEEDING
MAP OVERLAY 3 X 1630 HOURS

OFFICIAL DESIGNATION OF SENDER          TIME SIGNED   1645

AUTHORIZED TO BE SENT BY RADIO OR VISUAL IN:
CLEAR......                    SIGNATURE AND RANK OF WRITER   SGT
MOD CLEAR......                GPO 16—30938-4
SIGNATURE OF OFFICER

and Navajo and a minimum weight of 122lb, and be in overall good health and physical condition. The primary hurdles were fluency in English and the weight requirement. Many Navajo spoke only "trader English," and code talker Jimmy King later recalled that many Navajo recruits were eliminated due to limited education, particularly in spelling. The average American male of that era weighed about 150lb, but the Navajo were smaller both from genetic factors and from malnourishment stemming from poverty on the reservation. The age requirement was easy to circumvent. Birth records on the reservation were somewhat irregular, and the recruiter often had to take the applicant's word about his date of birth.

Recruitment was slow at first because the Marines had rejected many BIA suggestions, and that bureaucratic institution was offended. The paternalistic BIA had a tendency to treat its charges like overgrown children. After the chairman of the Tribal Council notified the various agency stations by the short-wave radio that substituted for telephones in the desert, applications increased rapidly. Some, like the unemployed Carl Gorman, thought perhaps they would secure a comfortable job in Washington, wearing a set of dress blues every day. Winston Chee had little trouble enlisting.

Carl Gorman, age 35, simply told them he was 29. William Dean Wilson was only 16 years old. "At noon the recruiters had gone to lunch, and we were left in the hall. We were mingling around there, and I saw this stack of folders on the recruiter's desk, mine sitting way off at the side, tagged with information that parents won't consent. I gently pulled it (the tag) out, and put it (the folder) underneath the big stack." Others utilized common ruses. "Feather merchants" gorged themselves on bananas, and drank enormous quantities of water or milk before officially weighing in, a practice to which many recruiters turned a blind eye.

Winston Chee's parents arranged a Blessing Way ceremony before he departed. This two-day ceremony, with its basis in the creation myth, was intended to restore the balance in his life, which the Navajo believe is the basis of well-being. On the first night an old *yata'ali'i* sang the sacred songs through the dawn hours, followed the next day by a ritual bath in water and soap made from the sap of the yucca plant. Winston donned new clothing and gifts of jewelry from his family. More prayer and song, and the creation of the sacred paintings from pollen, corn meal, and dried flowers, followed. The second night concluded with another all-night singing including the Twelve Word Song, with its sacred words pleasing to the ancient Holy People. The *yata'ali'i* presented Winston with a buckskin bag to wear around his neck, containing a supply of corn pollen to be used in morning prayers. His parents received an eagle feather, tied into a knot, to hold as insurance against his return.

Alex Williams Jr described his own ceremony: "See, there's a whole bunch (of feathers) tied and then they sprinkle you with water and the medicine herbs they usually put in, when you take a bath and all that."

On the afternoon of May 4, 1942, the recruits were sworn into the Marine Corps at Fort Wingate. After swearing to bear true allegiance to the United States of America the group boarded a chartered bus for San Diego.

The unexpected success of the first recruits assured the continuance of the program. Other recruits would flow into the recruiting pipeline, and over 400 Navajo would serve in the code program. The real limitation on recruiting would continue to be proficiency in English. Many families would not send their children away to the boarding schools, and schools on the reservation were all too often substandard.

It is worth noting that patriotic fervor was no less strong among the other tribes. Some had enlistment rates as high as 70 percent of the eligible male population despite the typical disqualifications due to low weight, poor health, illiteracy, and diseases such as tuberculosis.

Unlike the Marines, the Army bureaucracy continued to resist the idea of code talkers. Their experts cited the fact that both Japanese and German scholars had studied Native languages, and said that captured code talkers might be forced to send false messages. Military intelligence and the FBI were aware that suspicious "anthropology students" from both countries had studied native languages but without much success. They completely ignored the fact that many enemy combatants spoke fluent and idiomatic American English, and that white soldiers could just as readily be coerced into sending false messages. The US Navy used only a small number of code talkers for regional aircraft operational communications.

There was also recruitment amongst other Native American tribes. Comanche Nolly Bird was recruited while a 17-year-old senior at a boarding

These soldiers at Camp Benning, Georgia, in April 1941 are wearing the blue denim "fatigue" uniform. Every other man has an M1903 rifle, and the others are using wooden poles for bayonet training. (NARA)

Publicity photo of Comanche code talkers of the 4th Signal Company, Camp Benning, 1941. The men are wearing the woolen combination dress-combat uniform. Most, like the man at the far right, carry wire cutters/pliers in a light tan canvas belt pouch. (NARA)

school. In December 1940 Bill Karty came to see Nolly at his home in southeastern Oklahoma during the school's Christmas holiday. Karty was evasive but insistent. Most of the community was familiar with the Army code program from World War I, so Karty's work was an open secret. Nolly's mother refused Karty's blandishments, but a few days later Nolly turned 18, dropped out of school, and enlisted. In the short interim before he reported for training, one of Nolly's uncles arranged for a traditional farewell ceremony, including the singing of the old Soldier Society songs remembered from times when the Comanche were the curse of white settlers on the frontier.

## TRAINING

Nolly Bird reported to Camp Benning, Georgia, in early 1941, with a small group of Comanche who would be the Army's only formally organized code talkers. The informal head of the group was Charles Chibitty, last surviving descendant of a hereditary chief. All joined the 4th Signal Company, 4th Infantry Division.

Basic training was hasty, conducted within the newly created division. Two drill sergeants, Clifford Rate and John Boozer, were more surprised than their recruits. All but one student had spent years in the government boarding schools where students marched to and from class, made their bunks military style, and even told the hours in military time. Basic training was reduced from six weeks to two.

In August Nolly was sent to Louisiana with other members of the division, to spend several weeks slogging through the countryside on an elaborate field exercise. On a few occasions he sent and received routine messages in Comanche.

After returning to Camp Benning the recruits were reequipped with modern uniforms and weapons, and assigned to develop a code based on their language. The officer in charge did not speak the language, so the enlisted men developed a code, making up names for military equipment and terms. About 250 words or phrases were simply substituted, like "pregnant bird" for bombing plane. The code talker prefaced each message by saying *Meekununa*, "Listen to me." Unfamiliar words could be spelled out using Comanche equivalents, such as *aniku'ura*, or ant, for A, *saddi*, or dog, for D.

The division rotated through specialized training camps. Ultimately the 4th Signal Company was carried to the docks in Hoboken, New Jersey, in great secrecy, and embarked for England, arriving in Liverpool on January 29, 1944.

Nolly's closest brush with death in fact came during his training, on Operation *Tiger*, a practice landing in southern England. On the night of April 28, 1944, he was aboard an LST plodding along toward a simple administrative landing. One of the escort ships had developed engine trouble, but no one was particularly concerned.

Without warning the LST in the column ahead exploded, knocking the men in the cargo deck off their feet. A pack of German E-boats from France had come to investigate the unusual radio traffic generated by the practice assault earlier in the day. A second ship exploded as another torpedo struck home. Panicky sailors opened fire with all weapons at real and imagined targets.

The eerie shriek of the single escort ship's siren, tracers arcing through the black night, screams, and the flames of dying ships rattled Nolly as no other thing ever would. He strapped on his inflatable life belt, actually little more than a bicycle inner tube, and started up the steep ladder to the top deck. Halfway up the ladder an errant 20mm cannon round came through the ship's thin side and struck a glancing blow on the front of his helmet, spinning it around. The round failed to explode.

Nolly tumbled down on top of other soldiers, bleeding profusely from a torn scalp. He became the first man in his unit to win a Purple Heart – and became the butt of numerous bad jokes about being scalped by the Germans. The so-called Slapton Sands episode was shrouded in security, leading to the myth of a "cover up."

\* \* \*

The original group of Navajo recruits formed the 382nd Recruit Platoon, about half the size of a normal recruit platoon. This allowed the Drill Instructors (DIs) to devote special attention to each recruit. One of the recruits, Eugene Crawford, had experienced military life through the Reserve Officer Training Corps, and aided the others

Constant training and retraining were a major part of a code-talker's life in the Pacific as the men were called upon to perform new duties, and new versions of the code were introduced. Corporal Lloyd Oliver instructs privates first class Peter Nahaidinae and Joseph P. Gatewood at the Amphibious Scout School in June 1943. (NARA)

in adjustment to the alien world. John Benally said that in the old BIA boarding schools "… We marched to wherever we went to, school or to classroom or to the dining hall or to churches in formation. We knew how to drill, you know, not in the real military fashion, but we knew how to drill."

The spartan conditions were a holiday for those accustomed to desert poverty. The relative abundance of food allowed the recruits to gain weight and strength, though the alien diet often disagreed with the digestion of men accustomed to a diet of corn, mutton, and simple vegetables.

The Marine Corps was determined that the recruits would conform to all aspects of Marine training, which was harsher, both physically and mentally, than Army training. No allowances would be made for cultural differences, nor was training to be shortened for any reason. Winston, like many others, found the cultural shock disconcerting. DIs stared into the recruit's eyes at close range while screaming in outrage at some shortcoming. Both practices were virtually unknown in Navajo society.

Training was thorough, including drill, rifle and pistol marksmanship, hand-to-hand combat training, survival on land and in the water, and physical labor. The Corps was constructing its training facilities, and recruits provided free labor.

Marine Corps marksmanship training was quite difficult, with smaller targets at longer ranges than was typical of most armies. The Corps also preferred to teach recruits their own version of the special skills of rifle marksmanship, with many specialized (and often uncomfortable) body positions designed to hold the rifle steady for long-range fire. Many in the 382nd Recruit Platoon were accustomed to hunting small game or shooting at coyotes that threatened the family's sheep, while conserving costly ammunition. The recruits took to the marksmanship training with a vengeance, and the group as a whole achieved higher than average marksmanship qualifications.

Civilian habits were broken by novel measures. Wilfred Billey recalled that his DI cured his recruits of standing with their hands in their pockets by having them fill the pockets with sand and sew them shut.

The Navajo recruits were subjected to the usual indignities and suffering: digging holes and refilling them, scrubbing the heads (Marine slang for toilets), and for the 382nd Platoon, bathing Sergeant Duffy, the bulldog mascot of the training command. The Navajo recruits were in some ways exemplary, with a zero incidence of recruits being sent back in training for failure to master certain skills.

Communications school included a variety of curricula, but many hours were spent in learning Morse. The system was a significant hurdle for many Navajo. The PFC instructor is keying a message in dots and dashes; the students receive and type out the message. (NARA)

This staged photograph shows Corporal Henry Bake Jr (L) and Private George H. Kirk (R) with their TBY radio outside its canvas pack. Kirk is armed with the "airborne" version of the Reising submachine gun. (NARA)

Immediately after graduation the recruits were sent to Camp Elliott, and on Monday, June 29, given a brief lecture on military codes and told that they would be responsible for developing a code. Security was pervasive. They could not discuss their work with outsiders, even if asked by the most senior officers. Trips to the head would require an escort. Unusually for the military, there was no appointed leader. The Navajo would work democratically, and report their progress as a group.

According to Carl Gorman they were shown copies of various codes used by the other services. Gorman said that since the Navajo have no alphabet, they simply translated the English alphabet. By some accounts Wilsie Bitsie suggested they start with a simple alphabet. Oscar Ilthma's father had described to him the spoken letter code – Able, Baker, Charlie, etc. By the end of the day the group had worked out a simple alphabet code. English and Navajo words were different in sound. B became *shush* (bear). For example "code" would be "*moasi/ ne-ahs-jah/ bel dzeh*" – cat/owl/deer/elk.

Inventors of the Navajo code also substituted common words for terms that did not occur in their language. Grenades became potatoes, a route a rabbit trail, a flare a light streak, and a torpedo a fish shell. Inevitably, Army soldiers were dog-faces. Three more Navajo, college educated, were brought in to help with more abstract terms.

The men pored over manuals and developed a 211-word vocabulary of new words, which added to the complexity of the code. *Ne-ahs-jah*, owl, might represent either the letter O, or an observation plane, depending upon the context. Many terms were not intuitively obvious. Organizational elements were named for clans; a division was a "salt" (the *Ashi'ihi* or Salt People), and a platoon a "mud" (the *HashtX'isbni'i* or Mud People).

There was also considerable emphasis on speed. Not only were rapid communications desirable, it was also emphasized that long transmissions made it possible for the enemy to locate the transmitter.

Communicators received additional combat training, and all the curricula of the usual signals course. The men learned Morse, semaphore flag signaling, panel codes (laying out panels of colored cloth to communicate with aircraft in the absence of a radio), and the use and maintenance of field telephones, long-range and short-range radios, and telephone switchboards.

While the first group was in training the 1st Marine Division landed on Guadalcanal and nearby islands to capture bases the Japanese were building, from which they could sever the sea lanes to Australia. For the Allies, Australia was vital. It would be the springboard from which they could retake the Philippines, and cut Japan off from the resources of the East Indies.

In the early morning hours of August 9 the Japanese retaliated. Japanese cruisers and destroyers slipped unseen among the Allied shipping off Guadalcanal. In less than quarter of an hour four cruisers were sunk, another crippled. The transport ships fled southward, taking with them food, ammunition, construction equipment, and artillery pieces. The horrific struggle for Guadalcanal had begun.

The campaigns in the Southwest Pacific jungles – Guadalcanal, New Georgia, Bougainville, and New Britain – would soon prove to be precisely the type of fighting that the code program was designed to support. Both sides could readily listen in on each other's long-range radio messages and tap into their opponent's telephone lines in the trackless jungles. The ability to communicate quickly, accurately, but above all securely would provide critical tactical and strategic advantages.

When they completed training John Benally and Johnny Manuelito stayed at Camp Elliott to teach the next class of code talkers. The rest immediately shipped out to join I Marine Amphibious Corps. From there some would be sent to the 1st Marine Division fighting on Guadalcanal, some to garrison units scattered about the southern Pacific, and others to the 2nd Marine Division.

The Corps had approved a massive expansion of the program. Several blind tests conducted by skeptical generals had demonstrated that the code talkers could relay complex messages, error free, in a fraction of the time required by the mechanical coding machines. A group of cryptographers spent three weeks trying to break the code, eventually giving up in frustration. The Director of Plans and Policies asked the Commandant to authorize immediate recruitment of 200 more Navajo.

**B**   **TRAINING USMC CODE TALKERS, CAMP ELLIOTT, CALIFORNIA, 1942**

The new Navajo "code within a code" was shrouded in great secrecy, and even senior generals were not privy to the secret. The code talkers were authorized to deliver a translated message only to a limited group of approved officers and NCOs. These men are some of the first code talkers, working to develop the code using the simplest of tools – a chalkboard and typewriter. The heavily guarded room was located at the end of a long hallway in one of the hastily constructed buildings at the new camp. For security the first code talkers were largely segregated from other Marines, and could not even go to the head (latrine) alone. Development of the code was a most un-military undertaking. With no officers or senior NCOs who spoke the language, the small group of privates and PFCs had little choice but to work cooperatively as a group of equals. Later an additional code center was established in Hawaii. No written copy of the code was allowed outside of these heavily guarded rooms. The code and all of its complex vocabulary were committed entirely to memory.

Consideration was given to enlisting white speakers, but non-Native speakers had little mastery of the language. Code talker Jimmy King recalled:

> ... some of the white boys thought that they knew the Navajo language. They were born out here on the Navajo Reservation in some of these trading posts. Their parents were Indian traders and they were brought up among the Navajos, with the Navajos. They played with the Navajos during their childhood. They picked up the language so well. But never well enough that they could pass the test to be one of the code talkers. They spoke the language like coffee, flour, and counting of money. They knew how to say that, but there was always a fraction of a syllable that they could not pronounce exactly, and as exact and precise as it should be, so there would be no maybe and if about it. Some places there were words they had never heard. All they knew was known as trading post language ... But they could not carry on a conversation outside of the Navajo trading post language.

Philip Johnston was anxious to work with the program he had helped create, and applied to the commandant. On October 2, 1942, he was specially inducted with the rank of staff sergeant. Johnston was assigned to special duties only, to act as a liaison between the Navajo recruits and the white command structure. Direct inductions without recruit training were extremely rare at the enlisted level. There are other peculiarities surrounding Johnston's induction that are lost to history; normally an older college-educated man with a specialty like civil engineering would have been directly inducted as an officer.

Later recruits received the benefits of more systematic training. New recruits were included in the regular training platoons of the Recruit Depot. Philip Johnston, however, was assigned to Camp Elliott to help plan the second training cycle for code talkers. His command of the language was not sufficient to act as a trainer, but he served as a liaison between the Navajo instructors and higher commands.

The code training became more systematic. The first two phases of three weeks each were devoted to learning the code and simple translation skills. In the first phase students memorized the alphabet and the 211-word military vocabulary. Manuelito and Benally would call out the code words, and the students would translate into written English. In the second phase instructors translated military messages into Navajo, and read them aloud for the students to translate back into English. Students were repeatedly drilled until all exhibited the speed and accuracy desired.

Students then spent two weeks in field exercises in the dusty hills. This phase was devoted to learning the use and maintenance of the communications tools that would enable them to call down artillery, naval gunfire, and tactical aircraft. Practice with encoding, transmitting, and decoding messages continued through this practical phase. The Camp Elliott cryptologist, Capt Stilwell, monitored their message traffic, looking for weaknesses in the code.

At the end of the school session the two instructors shipped out to join the Fleet Marine Force in the Pacific, and four of the second-cycle students stayed behind as instructors. They incorporated Stilwell's suggestions, designed to make the code less vulnerable to code-breaking techniques. Many of these code-breaking techniques were statistical. The vowel E is the most common letter in written English, followed by T, A, O, I, and N. To break a simple substitution code like Shackle, the code-breaker simply analyzes a large number of messages, and examines the number of occurrences of each substitution. Thus the most common word – *dzeh* – would be the English E. Capt Stilwell suggested that for E, and the other most common letters in English, at least three words were to be used and switched randomly. Eventually at least three different word substitutions were used for each of the 18 most commonly used letters. Stilwell recommended that additional whole-word substitutions be used to further thwart statistical analysis, and 200 more words entered the vocabulary. The vocabularies and substitutions developed by each class were adopted by units already in the Pacific through constant retraining. Units in the field also developed unique code names for particular enemy bases and units, tactical objectives, tactical phase lines, and many other terms.

Paul Blatchford entered the Marine Corps in May 1943. He had extensive experience in communications, operating the two-way radio network for the BIA in Window Rock, New Mexico. After initial training he was assigned to the University of Omaha for an advanced electrical engineering course. As he was to board the train, he was pulled out of line by two NCOs and asked to go instead to Pendleton. "... we want you to go over there and be an instructor, and teach these Navajos how to maintain these radios, in case they're out on the front lines and their radios should go out. Teach them just the minor repair work." Blatchford was offered an instant promotion to private first class (PFC), but never told that the university training would have meant an officer's commission.

Blatchford worked with Philip Johnston, learning the code from his students in his spare time. He grew increasingly frustrated with failure to obtain promotion or a transfer to a combat unit. He was promised a transfer when the flow of trainees slackened, but "It didn't look it. There were more then, just coming in, and I thought 'Gee, we'll never get through with this.'"

On the advice of another Marine, Blatchford decided to go AWOL, on the theory that he would be sent overseas as punishment. He simply failed to return from liberty in town, and hitchhiked as far as Flagstaff, Arizona. Before reaching home, he decided to return because it was cold and he had already been absent long enough to get into trouble. When he returned to the town near the camp's main gate, he met up with a group of women Marines, and spent the rest of the day idling with them. He returned to the base with the women aboard their bus, entering unquestioned through the main gate.

".... I was teaching class about ten o'clock and the MPs [military police] came and got me, took me. No, they didn't take me to the brig. They took me right straight to the colonel." The colonel didn't believe the story of how Blatchford had gotten back aboard the base, but instead accepted an elaborate story he made up about sneaking past sentries. True to tradition, Blatchford was offered the chance to avoid brig time by volunteering to go to the new Reconnaissance Company, 5th Marine Division. Within two weeks he was a corporal in the Recon Company.

Vernon Begay, an older married man who had lived among the whites for years, entered with the third class. School was a torment for Vern. He possessed an outstanding command of both Navajo and English, but lacked formal education. The instructors were perfectionists who knew the lives of Marines might depend upon the speed and accuracy of messages. The students were graded on English spelling and penmanship, and instructor Jimmie King was always after Vern about his handwriting. Vern eventually passed the course and moved on to the Fleet Marine Force. The failure rate for Navajo communicators was only about 5 percent.

# APPEARANCE AND EQUIPMENT

Both Comanche and Navajo communicators were dressed and equipped exactly like their non-Native fellows. Despite their unique role, the only thing that set them apart physically was their racial characteristics, and even these were sometimes minimal. In the European theater the GI wore a variant of the dress uniform into combat.

The details and procurement schedules of the various combat utility uniforms worn by Marines are described in more detail in *US Marine Corps Raider 1942–1943* (Warrior 109). Uniform clothing and web gear were more distinctively "Marine" than weapons and were manufactured by the Corps' own depots.

Telephone communications gear had not really changed much since World War I, as illustrated by this shot of a typical wire team, taken just after the Guadalcanal Campaign. At this time the code talker program was shrouded in extreme secrecy, and photos of them were simply not taken. (NARA)

In late 1941 the Marine Corps adopted the distinctive cotton Utility Uniform, HBT, Sage Green, P1941 as the standard combat uniform. HBT (Herring Bone Twill) cloth was more durable and versatile, and better suited to conditions in the Pacific. The P1941 uniform was solid color, though the texture of the cloth imparted a subtle striped appearance. The trousers had two patch pockets on the seat, and two internal pockets on the front. They came in only one length, and individual Marines typically hacked off the extra fabric, leaving a ragged end to the leg. The matching jacket (shirt) had three patch pockets, one on each breast and another on the right side of the skirt.

Footgear was boondockers, low-top boots of russet brown suede leather with a black rubber

## **C** WEAPONS AND EQUIPMENT OF USMC CODE TALKER, PACIFIC WAR, GUADALCANAL AND BOUGAINVILLE CAMPAIGNS, 1942–43

The Marine Corps used an assortment of weapons and equipment in the early Solomon Islands jungle campaigns, some of it not well suited to the jungle conditions. The most common personal weapon of the code talkers was the Reising submachine gun (**1**), a lightweight but often unreliable weapon. The elaborate muzzle compensator was intended to keep the muzzle from rising during fully automatic firing. Its primary virtue was that it was immediately available. The M1903 rifle (**2**) with its long 16-in. bayonet was the preferred weapon because of its reliability and accuracy. The "airborne" version of the Reising gun with its folding wire stock and simplified muzzle compensator (**3**) was also widely used by the code talkers. The heavy Kabar ™ fighting knife (**4**) was a distinctive weapon for Marines, though it was more often used for such utilitarian tasks as opening cans and cutting wire. The M1 Lensatic Compass with its russet leather belt pouch (**5**) was an essential item for navigation in the dense jungle. The TBY "Walky-Talky" (**6**) was adapted from a Navy emergency radio, and was the standard short-range tactical radio of the Marine Corps. It was powered by rechargeable batteries carried in a box strapped beneath the main radio unit, and could be fitted with either a telephone handset or the more common headphones and throat microphone shown here. The TBY in its canvas backpack is also depicted (**7**). The Field Document Case (**8**) was used to carry maps, writing materials, and other materials used by officers, communicators, and observers. Shown inside the case are the clear gridded acetate map overlay that could be marked with grease pencils, and a book of field message blanks. The heavy, bulky TBX long-range radio (**9**) was another modified ship's radio, shown here in its waterproof case. Below is the field accessory box (**10**), used to carry spare vacuum tubes, parts, and tools. The bulky TBX Radio Accessory Trunk (**11**) was carried by each long-range communications team. Below it are the battery charger and testing unit (**12**). The inflatable rubber life belt (**13**) was worn during assault landings. It could be inflated by compressed gas, or by mouth using the black rubber tube. Heavily burdened Marines who went into the water found the lifebelt something of a macabre joke.

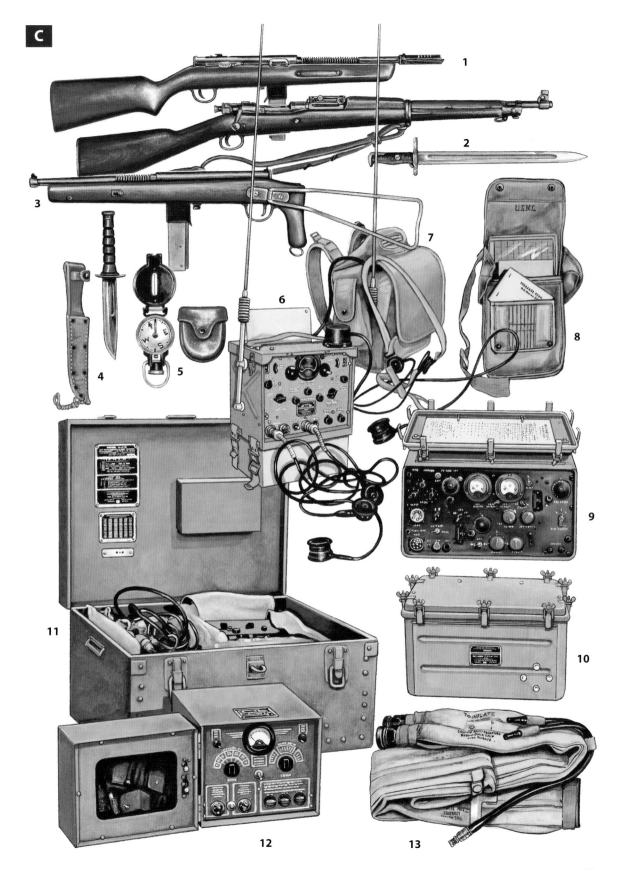

sole. Canvas gaiters were worn over the boots. These were another item of unique design, higher and made of a distinctively lighter tan canvas. Many Marines either wore the trouser legs loose over the tops of the leggings, or discarded the leggings altogether.

Web gear – packs, ammunition belts and pouches, canteen pouches, first aid kits, etc – were similar to Army patterns, but manufactured by the Corps' own suppliers. Marine Corps items were made of a slightly lighter khaki (tan in European usage) material than Army gear. Two distinctive items were the canteen pouch, which had extra long closure flaps that formed an X shape, and the blue-enameled steel canteen. Later model web gear items were indistinguishable from those of the Army.

The Uniform, Utility, HBT, Camouflage, P1942 uniform appeared after the Guadalcanal campaign, and became the most common field uniform. The P1942 uniform was reversible, with one side dominated by browns (beach), the other by greens (jungle). The reversible design meant that the accessible pockets were reduced to two on the jacket (left breast and right skirt) and two on the trousers (right front and left hip). Many Marines simply slashed through the fabric to make the pockets on the reverse side accessible. This uniform also introduced the distinctive reversible cloth helmet cover.

The Marine Corps began the war with various models of the M1903 rifle, usually called the Springfield. The M1903 was a .30-cal. bolt-action rifle prized by the Marines for its accuracy, and the standard weapon of the Marine infantry through most of the Guadalcanal campaign. In late 1942 the M1 Garand, a heavier semi-automatic .30-cal. weapon, began to replace the M1903. When the first code talkers arrived on Guadalacanal, the M1903 was still the standard there, so many of these men trained with the M1 but used the M1903 in service.

Communicators carried heavy radios, field telephones, and reels of wire, and so were often issued lighter weapons. In the early campaigns Reising submachine guns were common. The inexpensive Reising was adopted by the Marines simply because it was available. It came in two versions. The standard

Publicity photos of the code talkers gradually began to be released, though their exact role was not described. This group photo was taken on Bougainville in December 1943. (NARA)

version had a wooden stock and a complex muzzle compensator. The airborne version had a folding wire stock, and a simplified muzzle compensator.

The Reising was replaced by the more reliable M1 carbine. This lightweight weapon was not popular with the infantry, as the Marines thought it lacked the stopping power of the M1, and was not considered as reliable. Its reduced weight made it an ideal weapon for a heavily burdened communicator.

Another weapon issued to communications personnel was the Riot Gun, a militarized 12-gauge pump-action shotgun. The M12 and M97 Riot Guns differed from their civilian counterparts in having a carrying sling and a lug for mounting a bayonet. Special 00, or "double-ought," buckshot brass-cased ammunition was provided, as standard paper cartridges would not withstand field conditions. The Riot Gun was a fearsome weapon at close range, firing a spray of lead pellets. A skilled user could fire the weapon as fast as an automatic rifle and it was a popular weapon.

The M1911 .45-cal. automatic pistol was more common among communications personnel, though it was typically an officer's weapon. Though it was a beastly weapon to fire because of the powerful recoil, a hit anywhere in the torso or limbs would typically disable an enemy.

The true weapons of the code talkers were radios and telephones, which they could use to call down firepower ranging from artillery and aircraft to the 16-in. guns of battleships. At the beginning of World War II field telephones were still the most tactically mobile and reliable means of battlefield communication. Field radios were bulky, delicate, and fairly fragile because of the glass vacuum tubes. Most were AM (Amplitude Modulated), and prone to interference by static (electronic noise) produced by static electricity, weather, and the ignition systems of vehicles or aircraft. Water was an ever-present problem in amphibious landings and jungles. The radios could not be effectively waterproofed because they needed ventilation to cool the vacuum tubes, yet the slightest amount of moisture was often fatal. The US military and electronics industry later developed FM (Frequency Modulated) radios, which provided static-free communications.

The standard field telephone in the early days of the war was the Navy MCT-1, a sound-powered telephone carried in a waterproof canvas bag. The Army counterpart, which soon replaced it in Marine Corps service, was the EE-8 or EE-8A. Elaborate telephonic networks could be established using portable field switchboards, and the BD-72 type was common in Marine Corps service. The field switchboard allowed an operator to manually make cross-connections, quickly connecting forward observers directly to artillery positions.

Field telephones remained the most reliable communications systems throughout the war, at all levels. The negative aspect of field telephones was that it was often dangerous to lay wire into front-line positions. Looking after the thousands of miles of wire that festooned the typical battlefield was a maintenance nightmare, as it was constantly ripped apart by shellfire and vehicle traffic. Maintenance of the wire network was a dangerous task, as the wireman was required to move about day or night, under shellfire, and even in enemy-held ground to locate and splice breaks.

The original field radios were the TBX series, -1 through -8. TBX was a Navy code indicating "semi-portable radio equipment of low power." TBXs were designed for various types of communications, and the designation indicated the use, such as land-to-ship. John Benally reported that "... they were pretty heavy. It took two men to carry, two units, plus the generating unit. But any small repair or anything in these particular radios ... we knew how to just more or less trouble shoot in case there was something (wrong). We had a check list to go through, see what was wrong with the radio..." The advantage of the TBX was power and range, providing voice communications over hundreds of miles, and it could send and receive Morse key messages over even greater ranges.

The much smaller TBY backpack radio was a Navy designation for "portable radio equipment of low power used as emergency for TBS" (Talk Between Ships). In World War II the term "walky-talky" referred to this radio. The TBY's main disadvantage was limited battery life. John Benally explained: "The walky-talkies, you had to be very careful that, when you do receive, you have a certain pre-determined time to turn them on or off."

The first truly man-portable tactical FM radio was the SCR300, introduced in 1943. Also nicknamed the "walky-talky," the SCR300 was a backpack FM radio that used either a telephone-type handset or headphones and a microphone. Effective range was 10–20 miles. Batteries attached to the bottom of the radio provided 16–20 hours of continuous service. It weighed

The backpack TBY radio was a vast improvement in battlefield communications, but the antenna waving above the operator's head made him a natural target for enemy snipers. This poor quality and grainy photo is one of the few that shows an early code talker in action on Bougainville. (NARA)

32lb with the lighter battery, 38lb with the preferred heavier battery. The usual antenna was the AN-130-A, which protruded 33in. above the top of the radio. A 128-in. antenna, the AN-131-A, gave longer range and better signal quality. This antenna, broken into sections, was carried in a separate case. Additional gear such as the repair kit, spare vacuum tubes, and other items added to the communicator's burden.

Later in the war the Marines also used the new SCR536 "handie-talkie" or "spam can" hand-portable AM radio. The SCR536 was the first truly portable tactical radio. To turn it on the user pulled out the antenna; pushing in the antenna turned the radio off. Though lightweight (5lb) it was fairly sturdy, and could survive brief immersion in water. Range of the SCR536 was limited to a maximum of 3 miles and was usually line-of-sight only. Like all AM radios it was vulnerable to interference.

# BELIEF AND BELONGING

For the Army or Marine recruit patriotism, Nazi atrocities, and most of all the surprise attack on Pearl Harbor, were immediate motivating factors. The Marine Corps' publicity machine, particularly the reputation for being the "First to Fight," made it the service of choice for those who wanted to get at the enemy the fastest way possible. The Army recruit was equally motivated by patriotism, but the Army did not in general place such high emphasis upon the organization.

If he proved physically and mentally suitable, the Marine recruit was invited to try for membership in what the Marine Corps itself considered the world's premier fighting force. The sobering "audition" for Marine Corps membership was seven weeks of boot camp.

More than any other branch of service, the Marines isolated their trainees. The isolation, and harshness sometimes amounting to outright brutality, made them into modern-day Spartans who believed that they were made to suffer more, make do with fewer resources, and be called upon to accomplish more results and make more sacrifices. This placed them in a world apart, and fostered an extreme institutional and personal pride often described as arrogance by members of sister services.

The much larger US Army could not afford to conduct such intensive training. In the prewar period and into 1942 Army training was often accomplished within the actual units in which the men would serve. Cadres of experienced men from existing units formed a hard core upon which the new unit was formed, and trained the new men in a very personalized way. In these units the men would train and fight alongside the same comrades, forming a long-lasting personal bond. Unlike the Marine Corps, the Army to a great extent practiced regional recruitment, so that an individual often felt that his performance reflected upon family and community.

The young Marine emerged from boot camp as a member of a proud brotherhood, the soldier a member of a much larger "band of brothers." In the stress of combat the soldier's or Marine's universe of loyalty quickly narrowed to those in his immediate unit. These were men who might be called upon to sacrifice their lives to save his; he might be called upon to make the same sacrifice. It was a bond of loyalty that transcended love. The young recruit might have enlisted out of patriotism, but in battle his loyalties were to his friends, his unit, his branch of service, and his country, in that order.

The new SCR300 provided far greater reliability and range not only for communications units, but for groups like this artillery control party of the 20th Marines on Saipan. (NARA)

For the Native American recruit the situation was more complex. Although they were a racial minority, there was almost no outright discrimination. Carl Gorman noted that, "The attitude was that we were Marines." For most tribes there was a strong warrior tradition, though only the elderly had any memory of battles against the US Army. In both World War I and World War II Native Americans enlisted in disproportionately large numbers, and served with distinction that was often not officially acknowledged.

For most tribes the situation was complicated by complex kinship systems. The various tribes were all fairly small in numbers, so that members were far more conscious of extended family relationships than in most societies.

The Navajo are a very large tribe, subdivided into 67 clans, or extended family groups. They have a complex social system intended to reduce the possibility of incest among a people living in thinly spread isolation. Each individual can trace his genealogy, and it is common for a Navajo to introduce himself by his name, and maternal and paternal clans, for example "Oscar Charley, born to the Salt People for the Towering House People." Accomplishments, or failings, of an individual reflect not only upon the individual but upon his extended family. This instills a powerful sense of duty.

Throughout their known history the Navajo have been farmers and herders, and they are not a particularly warlike people. Despite minor conflicts with neighboring tribes, and a prolonged struggle against the US Army that resulted in a brief and brutal exile, the *Dineh* have been resolutely pacifist. The Navajo religious belief system discourages violence of any sort, and considers warfare an aberration of nature. An individual who commits violent acts, even the government-sanctioned violence of war, is considered to have a "life out of balance." The basic essence of the religion is to restore and maintain that peaceful balance. Missionaries preaching the non-violent tenets of Christianity found that the Navajo easily accepted the new religion, which blended easily with the old ways.

Many individuals adopted some blend of Christianity and the older religion, though others continued to publicly downplay older beliefs. In many ways the older beliefs, built upon long experience with very personal warfare, better enabled veterans to cope with the horrors of the battlefield. Navajo Sidney Bedoni described the surprisingly sophisticated coping mechanism imparted by his people's "primitive" beliefs:

> Well, some people say that, well, it's something that you sacrifice, your mind. That's why they put (on) these ceremonies for you. It's not only a dance, but they have a way of doing it. And I guess that holds my mind together, I guess. You see, they say if you don't, why, your mind will be way over there, where you've been, all the time. Thinking about it. But since I had it done over me, why, I never thought of it."

Equally important in the Navajo social system is modesty to the point of self-effacement. In *Dineh* society special feats are achieved for the good of the people, not to garner acclaim for the individual. Anything that even remotely smacks of boastfulness or glory-seeking carries a powerful social stigma.

All these factors combined to produce a unique recruit population. These were men with a deep sense of duty that merged patriotism with deep familial loyalty, who did not seek battlefield glory but fought out of conviction, and who accepted that their achievements must remain a secret. They were ideal for the code talker program.

Unlike the Navajo, Comanche recruits were the inheritors of a long and powerful warrior tradition. Their ancestors hunted bison and raided across immense areas of the Southern Great Plains and as far south as Mexico. Comanche males were immensely proud of their martial skills, and individual bravery and accomplishments were highly praised. Inured to hardship, skilled in combat and field craft, and fanatically brave, they were formidable enemies. In their long conflict with the white settlers, the Army grudgingly called them "the best light cavalry in the world."

In their heyday Comanche males were typically members of a Soldier Society. Unique to Comanche society, these all-male fraternal groups recruited members, and membership in a Soldier Society crossed family and clan group boundaries. The members of the group trained, socialized, and fought together, and they were the best analog to a military unit in the white man's sense. The US government had taken stringent measures to suppress the Soldier Societies, but their ceremonies and traditions remained alive in the memories of the old men.

A common factor for all Native American recruits was personal friendship. Both the Army and Marine Corps drew recruits from already closely bonded tribes. The Marine Corps did not use a regional recruiting and service system, but in a relatively small organization within which men of similar background served in similar capacities, it was easy to keep track of your friends. The Army's regional recruitment system for the National Guard divisions meant that small groups of men grew up, enlisted, trained, and served together. Both organizations drew recruits from the vast deserts of Arizona and New Mexico and the sparsely settled Oklahoma Plains, where every other young man within a hundred miles was your "neighbor."

Another powerful bonding factor for both tribes was the old BIA school system. Many of the most promising youths spent their adolescence in far away boarding schools, where they became fluent in both English and their own languages. The atmosphere of the schools was often highly regimented, and discipline was unyielding. For these men there was the additional bond of a common, often harsh, school experience.

# THE EARLY PACIFIC CAMPAIGNS

### Daily life in the Southwest Pacific

The first Marine Corps unit deployed to the southwestern Pacific was a brigade sent to defend Polynesia against a possible Japanese invasion. Allied planners were still concerned that the seemingly invincible Japanese would move farther south to sever the critical routes to Australia and New Zealand. The balance of the 1st Marine Division followed later, and the Division assembled in New Zealand for the invasion of Guadalcanal. Preparations were chaotic, thrown into disarray by a dockworkers' strike. Specialized combat supplies had not yet been developed, and lashing rains ruined supplies like cardboard crates of corn flakes and toilet paper.

The first code talkers did not deploy with the division, since they were still in training, but crossed the Pacific like any other Marine. Winston Chee missed his assigned transport ship because of a brief illness, and traveled with a replacement draft. In 1942 specialized amphibious assault ships were still under construction, so most Marines traveled across the Pacific aboard old, slow troop transports. After departing California, most were cooped up aboard the ships for three or more weeks, with a brief stop in Hawaii for refueling and replenishing stores.

Life aboard a troopship was no pleasure cruise. The troops were quartered in berthing holds, with bunks stacked four or five high. The bunks were pipe frames covered with a wire mesh and a thin mattress. The frames were suspended by chains from the overhead, and could be folded up against a bulkhead or pipe frame. Gear was hung from the frames, with uniforms and a few personal items stowed in seabags. Showers and washing were done in salt water, and clothes were air dried. Newly laundered clothes, even underwear, were hard and scratchy to the skin.

Limited stores of fresh food were soon exhausted, and the cooks fell back on dry and canned foods. Meals were obtained by standing in long lines that snaked through passageways, and eaten standing up. Sometimes the lines were so long that the break between eating one meal and getting in line for another was only a couple of hours. On the monotonous diet and continuous regime of physical exercise most of the Marines, even the Navajo who had never lived a life of abundance, tended to lose weight.

In the tropical heat cooling was limited to air forced down vents by the slow progress of the ship. The Marines spent as much time as possible on the relatively cool weather decks, but at night when the ship was blacked out, they

PFC Hosteen Kelwood, Private Floyd Saupitty (a Comanche), and PFC Alex Williams aboard ship after the Peleliu operation. Note the inflatable rubber life belts. (NARA)

were confined below. Men lay in their bunks in the stifling holds. To turn over, they bumped against the wire supports of the bunk above, and heaved the weight of its occupant up to make space. Men were stacked in alternating rows, head-to-toe to minimize the spread of diseases, and the odors of feet, sweaty bodies, and intestinal gasses were pervasive.

There was little to do except sweat. It was an era when most men smoked, but smoking was limited to the daylight hours when the ship's loudspeakers announced "Now hear this, the smoking lamp is lit." The announcement was traditional, a holdover from sailing ship days when sailors lit their pipes from a special lamp.

The Marines were careful to field-strip their cigarette butts, letting the excess tobacco blow over the side, but holding onto the paper. Nobody wanted a trail of floating white paper that could alert enemy submarines to the ship's course. The paper, and all the rest of the ship's debris, was put into weighted bags and dumped over the side at night.

The men trained on deck – cleaning weapons, listening to lectures, and doing endless exercise to try to maintain their physical conditioning. Working parties helped sailors wash down decks, and did odd jobs to help maintain the aged ship. Books, specially printed pocket-sized novels, were passed around.

The primary event of the voyage was crossing the equator, with the associated Crossing the Line festivities. This was still a major event in the naval services, though jollities were reduced because of the necessities of war. On a troop ship most such ceremonies were also limited by the sheer number of

Marine communicators rest in a bunker on Guadalcanal. Both are wearing the Navy single headphone and chest-mounted microphone that could be hooked into radios or telephones. (NARA)

Pollywogs – new men – who had to be initiated. But on Winston Chee's voyage the ship's crew and the older Marines were determined to conduct a ceremony worthy of their ship.

On the great day Winston was dragged topside with a very large contingent of Pollywogs. Neptune's Court was dressed in peculiar improvised costumes, with old mops for hair and crowns made from odd bits of metal. The fattest sailor on the ship played the role of The Royal Infant, attired in a diaper made from a bed sheet.

Initiates were dragged forward dressed in their under shorts, hosed down with salt water, and dunked in a tub of swill from the galley. One by one they were asked a series of lunatic questions. Their attempts to answer were interrupted with howls of derision and mock rage. Chee was assessed a punishment to kiss The Royal Infant.

Four burly Shellbacks, sailors or Marines who had been initiated on prior voyages, grabbed Chee. With one man holding each limb, they shoved the struggling Chee's head into The Royal Infant's rolls of belly fat, which had been liberally slathered with thick gray propeller shaft grease. Chee was now a Shellback, complete with a printed certificate.

Winston finally joined up with the other code talkers at a forward staging base, and a week later boarded another ship, bound for CACTUS, the code name for Guadalcanal.

## Hastily into battle – the Solomons and Tarawa

When Winston Chee and the first contingent of code talkers from I Marine Amphibious Corps arrived on September 18, 1942, the 1st Marine Division was two months into the struggle for Guadalcanal. Marine Corps and Army Air Corps aircraft flying from the airfield contested enemy control of the skies, but at night the surrounding seas belonged to the Imperial Navy. American transport ships raced in just after dawn, frantically unloaded under attack from Japanese planes, and fled before nightfall. The large convoy included the first contingent of code talkers, desperately needed supplies, replacements for casualties, and most of all fresh reinforcements, the 7th Marines.

As Winston scrambled down the side of a Navy transport into a wooden LCP the Marine sergeant in charge shouted a ceaseless torrent of curses and threats to hurry them up. The sharp bark of long-range 5-in. antiaircraft guns on the escort ships was joined by the rapid hammering of 40mm guns. A few yards overhead the transport's own guns began to pound at the enemy planes. He let go of the rope net hanging down the ship's side, and plummeted into the boat as it took a drop in the waves. He landed heavily as the coxswain immediately gunned the boat engine and sheared away from the ship.

When the boat grounded in the shallow water, Winston rolled painfully over the side and landed on his knees. Scrambling to his feet he gathered up his gear and splashed up onto the black sand. All the Navajo were privates first class, so they just went on as a group through the scattered trees of a copra plantation, following the directions of a military policeman stationed near the beach.

No one believed that the group of privates and privates first class had orders to report directly to the division commander. The small contingent was sent inland, then back toward the beach. As they crossed a small clearing Winston heard the snarl of an aircraft engine. Tracers flashed across in front of him, and bullets kicked up mud and water. As the plane swept past he instinctively said, "*Da-he-tih'hi*. Hummingbird. Japanese Zero naval fighter," to no one in particular.

The group reported to a series of increasingly senior officers, and finally to a balding middle-aged man sitting at a folding field desk. The division commander, MajGen Alexander Vandegrift, noticed Winston's discomfort and had a nearby medical corpsman examine him while the others reported in. Short of medical supplies, the corpsman gave Winston a small white APC tablet.

Vandegrift was not expecting this odd group, and told them to report to his communications officer, Lt Hunt. By that time it was dark, so Hunt told them to find a place and stay in it. The hours of darkness were dangerous, more from trigger-happy sentries than from actual Japanese infiltrators.

Hunt trusted his coding machine more than the Navajo and devised his own test, one of the seemingly endless series demanded by various officers at all levels. Hunt dictated a message, and the code talkers transmitted and decoded it in two minutes. The results eventually convinced him that messages translated orally were not only as accurate as the mechanically encoded message, but could be sent and received in a few minutes rather than the four or more hours required by his machine.

Hunt dispatched the code talkers in radio jeeps to different parts of the perimeter, but no one had thought to warn the other communicators. When Winston spoke into the microphone for a radio check, another voice broke in. "Japs in the circuit." Within minutes the frequency was jammed. The division net was useless until Hunt broke in to silence the confusion.

In consultation with Hunt, the code talkers agreed that all transmissions in Navajo would begin with a code word, "Arizona" or "New Mexico," to indicate that the following message was in an American spoken code. The division's other communicators were advised that the broadcasts were legitimate, but not given any other information.

Winston was assigned to the Signal Company where he transmitted and received urgent radio traffic. He gradually learned to work, and even sleep, through the daytime air raids and the nocturnal bombardments by the Tokyo Express, the nickname given to the Japanese resupply attempts by their Imperial navy. Communications were mostly with regimental command posts, and occasionally unidentified ships lying offshore. As would be the case for most of the war, any message that was marked to be both encoded and labeled "Urgent" was sent in the Navajo code, since this was so much faster and more accurate than the mechanical coding machine. All messages marked "Secret" were also sent in the Navajo code, as it was considered the most secure code.

Ankle-deep black mud and the pervasive smell of rotting vegetation added another dimension of unpleasantness to life during the campaign. The supplies

**ABOVE LEFT**
When the first code talkers arrived on Guadalcanal, they had orders to report directly to MajGen Alexander Vandegrift, shown here at his headquarters. (NARA)

**ABOVE**
One of the mid-war Marine Corps innovations was the Joint Assault Signal Company, a team of Marines and Navy personnel who provided direct communications with naval gunfire support ships and aircraft. This team on Guam is using an old TBX radio. (NARA)

the Marines had brought ashore were exhausted, and the men were living off captured Japanese supplies. Already thin, Winston lost more weight on the unvarying diet. Two meals a day of rice, occasional canned fish, and a few rare and small servings of canned vegetables were sometimes augmented by an afternoon serving of rice pudding. Though troops at headquarters ate marginally better than the front-line infantry, and were not exposed to the debilitating exertion and worst living conditions, Winston suffered from skin rashes and diarrhea.

Most of all Winston hated the anti-malarial atabrine tablet, with its bitter taste and persistent aftertaste. Rumor had it that the pill made a man impotent. Many refused to take it, or surreptitiously spat it out. As malaria casualties soared, orders came down that NCOs would administer the drug at a daily "atabrine call."

Each evening the code talkers at the Signal Company lined up in front of the sergeant in charge. When his turn came, Winston opened his mouth wide and the sergeant tossed the little pill as far down his throat as possible, then had Winston take a drink of water from his canteen. Winston opened his mouth wide again so the sergeant could look for the pill, sometimes poking a grimy finger inside to make sure he had not secreted it away under his tongue or in his cheek, to be spat out later.

The code talkers were also sent deep into the jungle with reconnaissance patrols, since the language code could provide timely reports. One such patrol that included Sam Begay ran out of food and ammunition, but was guided to a hidden cache by another code talker inside the perimeter.

In the predawn hours of November 5 the sergeant shook Winston awake. "How's your leg, Chee?"

"Okay, sarge. Why?"

"Never mind. Just get your crap together. You're going on a hike."

Winston groaned. "Where?"

The sergeant fixed him with a cold stare. "You're gonna be gone for a while. Light marching pack."

Winston shoved a few items into his pack, and piled the rest of his gear together to await his possible return. He assembled the complex rig of belt suspender straps, knapsack, and web belt, and wandered out to stand with a few other dispirited men.

A few hours later Winston was in a landing boat, heading east along the coastline of Guadalcanal. After a few hours the boat turned into a broad bay, and scraped ashore near a large cloth beach marker panel. A grim-looking sergeant wearing a huge knife on his belt gathered them in, and led them past Navy construction troops. They reported to a gaunt, beak-faced man sitting under a tree. "This here's the other code talker, Colonel."

The commander of the 2nd Raider Battalion quickly outlined his mission. The battalion would break loose from its base, and march through the jungle to cut off Japanese troops reeling back from a defeated attack on the main perimeter. Winston would join Wilsie Bitsie, Eugene Crawford, Felix Yazzie, and Charlie Y. Begay, who had "volunteered" to join Carlson's unorthodox unit back on Noumea. Throughout the war code talkers would find themselves in units like Raiders, parachute battalions, and reconnaissance teams because commanding officers could simply requisition communicators or other specialists like any other piece of gear.

The code talkers provided rapid communication among the widely scattered units of Carlson's battalion, and with 1st Marine Division Headquarters. Carlson's enthusiasm and intensity reminded Winston of the Christian missionaries on the reservation.

Like the other code talkers Winston was assigned a bodyguard. Contrary to popular lore, the job of the bodyguard was not to kill the code talker to prevent his capture, but to assure that he remained alive and on duty.

Winston was attached to one of Carlson's infantry companies. The company patrols seemed to stumble about in the dank jungle, continually crossing streams and backtracking along their own path while every new day brought clashes with the Japanese. The Long Patrol, as Carlson's mission would be called, was a series of such clashes. For Winston the experience was particularly hideous. According to traditional Navajo beliefs, the *chindi*, or spirit of a recently deceased person, lingers about the death site and will sicken the living. Here the jungle stank of unburied Japanese bodies.

On the sixth night the company set up a position in a small village. Winston noted with relief that the houses were intact. At home a house where a person had died was abandoned, with one wall knocked out so that the *chindi* would depart. He started to dig a fighting hole, but in the darkness his shovel crunched against something hard and metallic. He gagged on a burst of foul gas that belched out of the hole. All around him other Marines were cursing and retching. The Japanese had buried hundreds of dead under the village, carefully hiding the graves. Winston abandoned the hole and slept lying on the ground, shivering in his wet clothing. Immersed in the smell of rotting flesh, his sleep was disturbed by vivid nightmares.

Winston was reeling with exhaustion and limping from the injury he suffered in the fall into the boat. The men inside the main perimeter were eating like kings compared to the Raiders. He had been raised on a diet of corn and mutton, and the military food had never agreed with his stomach. Now his diet was scarcely enough to maintain life itself. Worm-ridden rice was seasoned with salt and occasional bits of salted pork while a few raisins passed as vegetables.

Winston was racked by abdominal cramps and diarrhea, and weak from hunger. Still, he pressed on with the others, unwilling to let down his buddies.

If you could still stagger forward, you stayed and fought. At night he collapsed in the mud, sleeping through swarms of mosquitoes. Scratching the bites with his dirty fingernails created clusters of oozing sores. The corpsman rinsed them off with a little stream water, cleaned them with a bit of gauze, and painted them with antiseptic.

By early December Winston was a walking skeleton, shaking with chills and fever, hobbling along on an increasingly bad leg. Carlson decided to send half his force down the east bank of the Lunga River, while the less depleted companies continued over the slopes of Mount Austen.

As the Raider and Japanese patrols stumbled into each other, friendly fire was a very real problem. Winston's company was moving along the east bank of the river when 105mm artillery fire began to fall among them. The officer in charge of the patrol grabbed the radio handset and shouted into the voice radio "Artillery! Check fire! Check fire! You're firing on Marines!"

Another voice broke in "Ignore message. No friendlies that area."

"Damn it, you're firing on Marines!"

The shells continued to fall as the voice on the radio inquired "You got an Injun there?"

"Chief! Get the hell over here," shouted the lieutenant. "Get this fire lifted!"

Winston took the handset thrust into his face. He struggled to find the right words. "Arizona, Arizona. *Ashi-hi be-al-doh-tso-lani coh Has-clish-ni.*" Salt artillery firing on my Mud. "*Ni-da'than-zie be'na-ali-tsoisi.*" No turkey slant eyes (We are not Japanese). "*Na-hos-ah-gi' toh-ni-lin ...*" Near the stream ... Winston reeled off coordinates the officer had scrawled on a message blank. "*Jo-kayed-go' Ne-as-ja'* " We ask for an owl (Request aerial observation). Winston spelled out his last name for the code talker at the other end "*Moasi, lin, dzeh, ah-na'.*" Cat, horse, elk, eye. "*Ba'ha-this.*" Over.

"Understood." Within seconds the shelling stopped.

When the company entered the division lines, Winston was told to go on sick call. The corpsman mumbled a familiar litany: dysentery, ringworm, trench foot, conjunctivitis, non-specific tropical fever, jaundice, exhaustion, and an inflamed and swollen knee. Winston was given some more APC pills, a vitamin shot, and three days' rest in the infirmary. Then he was told to report back to the Division Signal Center for light duty. Men in such good condition would serve until replaced by fresh troops.

Code talkers would serve everywhere as the Marines fought their way up the Solomon Islands chain and they were invaluable in the jungle fighting on New Georgia and Bougainville in 1943.

As the Americans gradually gained superiority, things like food got better. Carl Gorman recalled the introduction of K-rations, dried foods packaged in

**USMC CODE TALKERS IN ACTION, BOUGAINVILLE, 1943**

This two-man communications team, part of an infantry battalion, is transmitting with the TBY backpack radio. They wear the early P1942 reversible camouflage utility uniform with the green, or "jungle," side out. The code talker on the left is armed with the M1 carbine that replaced the Reisng gun as a lightweight weapon for men who carried communications gear, heavy weapons, or other bulky equipment. The communicator wears the early pattern round, narrow-brimmed utility hat more common in the early war period. The radio is fitted with a telephone handset rather than the more common headphones and microphone. Both men wear round Marine Corps identity discs rather than the aluminum "dog tags" of the late war period. The man in the background is an infantryman assigned to provide security, and carries the new M1 Garand rifle. He is wearing the belt suspender straps that supported the weight of the web belt from the shoulders, and the older style canteen covers with crossed straps unique to the Marines.

D

37

The 2nd Marine Division at Tarawa utilized code talkers only in the 6th Marines. This is a typical CP on Tarawa, with a TBX radio at center. Antenna guy wires are barely visible, and the generator is clamped to a board between the men seated on the left. (NARA)

a box of heavily waxed cardboard. He later recalled that the only good thing was a big bar of chocolate.

The practice of appointing bodyguards for the code talkers seems to have been more a local initiative than policy. On Bougainville Bill Toledo, a code talker with the Headquarters Company, 3rd Battalion, 9th Marines was seized and held at gunpoint by men from one of the infantry companies in his own battalion. The battalion commander appointed a white communicator, Richard Bonham, as an unofficial bodyguard, primarily to protect Toledo against Marines who could not distinguish him from their Japanese enemies. Toledo was ordered not to go outside the battalion lines, and Bonham or a substitute was to accompany him at all times.

A later incident reinforced the wisdom of the system. One night on Bougainville code talker Harry Tsosie, one of the original code talkers, was shot by a Navy medical corpsman. He was the only one of the Original 29 to be killed, one of 11 code talkers killed during the war. Increasingly Marines were told to stay in place at night because anyone moving in the darkness was assumed to be a Japanese infiltrator, what the code talkers referred to as *na-as-tosi*, a stealthy mouse.

Despite the proven utility of the code talkers in the Solomons campaigns, they were still not universally accepted. Senior officers in the 2nd Marine Division declined to use the Navajo signalmen as intended. Thus when Dean Wilson's group of ten code talkers arrived at the 2nd Marine Division, rather than being distributed throughout the division, four went to the Headquarters Battalion and two each to the three battalions of the 6th Marines. The other two infantry regiments of the division and the division artillery would have no code talkers.

This photo, purportedly taken on Tarawa, shows a TBX radio, the generator clamped to the "idiot seat," and the heavy metal pole antenna. (NARA)

The 6th Marines were a holdover from previous Marine doctrine, specialists in landing from rubber boats. This earned them the sobriquet of the "condom navy." This was added to an existing nickname, "The Pogey Bait Marines," with which they were saddled after supposedly consuming a transport ship's entire supply of candy bars.

On the morning of the Tarawa landings in November 1943, Wilson snuck topside and hid under a boat cover to watch the shelling. As the division reserve, the 6th Marines escaped the carnage of the original landings, and landed intact along the east end of the island. As fresh troops, they played a major role in clearing the island's last defenders.

Wilson's rubber boat hung up on an obstacle, and he "... had to almost kind of half swim ashore" with his heavy gear. They were rushed forward until "... I fell in a hole, a shell hole where a dead Jap was lying. I got the shivers from it because I thought maybe he was still alive. Fortunately he wasn't. He was already dead." There was little demand for coded messages, only savage infantry fighting.

The heart of the field telephone system was any one of several models of field switchboard, like this one on Tarawa. By this period the typical weapon of communications personnel was the M1 carbine. (NARA)

Wilson's worst ordeal did not come in the battle, but afterward. If any place would be haunted by the *chindi*, it would be Tarawa. The 6th Marines were not as badly battered as the other regiments, so "We had to run around all over the place and find all the bodies we could find of our comrades, that we buried. I think about 500 that one morning." The bodies were bloated and blackened in the hundred degree (37.8 degrees Centigrade) heat. Many Marines wore gas masks to help with the stench. "They dug a huge trench about six or seven feet deep. We just laid these bodies in there, down in there, just stacked them, one on top of the other. That was quite a chore. I always thought of the Tarawa operation as that."

The final campaign on the "Solomons Ladder" was the capture of bases on western New Britain, to neutralize the huge enemy base at Rabaul. The 1st Marine Division, after recovering from the Guadalcanal ordeal, was assigned the task of seizing an airfield site at Cape Gloucester.

Cape Gloucester was the last of the true jungle fighting. There was still considerable concern about other Marines confusing the code talkers with Japanese, but such incidents were rare. The risk was greatest when the code talkers were functioning as runners, carrying hand-written messages. Jimmy King recalled: "We were runners, part of the time, being questioned and shot at by our own men."

One night the radio was out and the telephone was not functioning. King was sent out to trace the broken telephone line in the pitch-black jungle. He stumbled into another Marine, and blurted out the password "lame duck." He repeated the password but the other man, frightened, stuck a bayonet in his back, and was apparently going to fire when King luckily tumbled into a fighting hole occupied by a sergeant he knew. Suddenly firing broke out overhead, "... but I was down where I heard all of them being shot. Stayed there about half the night, I guess I was missing. They sent out some runners after me, and then they took me back ..."

A 1st Marine Division Signals Officer addresses a group of code talkers at the recuperation center on Pavuvu, following the Peleliu operation. All are wearing a mix of dress uniforms and boondocker field shoes. (NARA)

# THE CENTRAL PACIFIC CAMPAIGNS

## Daily life in a rest camp

Marine divisions in the Pacific spent long periods in base camps incorporating replacements, rebuilding shattered units, and allowing the men to recover from the effects of short but incredibly violent campaigns. Such camps might be at relatively luxurious places like Hawaii or Australia, or amid the swamps and coconut groves of advanced bases.

The survivors of the Guadalcanal Campaign were shipped to southeastern Australia, an ideal place to recover from the effects of the jungle. The cool climate alleviated the worst effects of malaria, and the men could fatten up on local food. Best of all was an English-speaking society where most of the younger men were away at war. The code talkers, like their comrades, struck up relationships with the locals, and some married and settled there after the war.

The troops were generally quartered in pyramidal squad tents, and slept on canvas folding cots under blankets. In the cool winter the Marines were issued field jackets to wear with their utility uniforms. The routine of daily life consisted of endless field exercises.

After Guadalcanal 1st Marine Division personnel recuperated and retrained in Australia. Gloves and field jacket are worn in the cool climate. The radio is a TBY. (NARA)

Because of the secrecy, senior officers were unaware of the code. One of the most troublesome aspects of a code talker's service was secrecy. A code talker serving at a command message center was authorized to deliver the decoded message only to the message center chief, or to an officer of lieutenant general rank or higher. This inevitably led to a PFC telling a colonel that he was not authorized to see a message.

After each campaign groups of Marines from various units were transferred out of the division for training or to provide cadres for new divisions. In mid-1943 Winston Chee was assigned to the code school at Pearl Harbor.

The purpose of such assignments was to learn new versions of the code that men could carry back to their unit in their heads. The code was constantly changed as a basic part of the security system. The code schools developed new variations on the code between each campaign, and men from the schools went out to the units in the field to teach the revised code. Each new code variant was documented, but code books never went west of Hawaii. There were only two physical copies of the code, one at Camp Pendleton and the other at Pearl Harbor. Both were kept under lock and key. In the field the code existed only in the minds of the men who used it.

To his dismay, Winston learned that on the day after Christmas, 1943, his division had invaded Cape Gloucester. For a Marine who had formed powerful bonds with his comrades this was a psychological blow. He requested immediate reassignment, but duty dictated that he would not rejoin the division for months.

After Tarawa, the 2nd Marine Division was sent to the largely agricultural "big island" of Hawaii. Units were housed all over the island, and on nearby Maui. The Parker Ranch training area was located on open, rolling ranchland high above the sea, in the saddle between two enormous volcanoes. The local agricultural economy was built around cattle and pineapples, of which the men grew heartily sick. The bulk of the diet consisted of canned and dried foods, and lots of bread.

Wilfred Billey found familiar entertainment. "They had rodeo, I remember, there, some of the Marine Corps participated. In fact, one Navajo – he rode in the rodeo there. Yes, his name was William Gilland."

The division command was determined not to repeat the Tarawa disaster. The Marines used tape and wooden stakes to lay out precise maps of the next objective, Saipan. On the open grazing land large units walked through their role in the assault. Formations walked along boat routes, across a tape "beach," spilled out of their "landing craft," and guided on major terrain features represented by more tape. The exercise was repeated, over and over, until each man knew his route and mission in detail.

After Cape Gloucester the 1st Marine Division went, not back to Australia, but to the island of Pavuvu in the Solomons, where the men had to construct their own camp. Swamps and rough terrain made parts of the small island useless for training. Infantry and tank training was conducted by

By the Marianas campaigns of mid-1944, communications had reached unbelievable levels of complexity, as illustrated by this 2nd Marine Division Message Center. Maintaining the snarls of wire was a major task. (NARA)

maneuvering through the camps themselves, dodging around the orderly ranks of trees in the copra plantations, and launching "assaults" through rows of tents. Artillery and tanks fired at imaginary targets in the sea.

Most Marines hated Pavuvu. Even sleep was disrupted by large land crabs that roamed the island, climbing into tents and cots. The troops seized upon almost any recreation. Alex Williams Jr recalled that on Pavuvu the 1st Division held a Navajo *Yebachia* dance directed against the enemy, sang Zuni war songs, and held traditional Comanche dances.

# LIFE ON CAMPAIGN

The 4th Marine Division's rapid capture of the twin islands of Roi-Namur in February 1944 came as a pleasant surprise to the Marine Corps leadership. Billy Chee landed with the division, but there was little need of sophisticated tactics or communications. The Navy and Marines were now positioned to launch themselves against the core of the Empire.

In many respects the campaigns of the southern Marianas in summer 1944 – Saipan, Tinian, and Guam – were the most strategically important of the Pacific War. The intense fighting was virtually ignored in the sea of publicity surrounding the Normandy campaign, but the capture of these islands placed long-range bombers and submarines within easy striking distance of Japan. The captured Territory of Guam also hosted the largest American civilian population to fall under the Imperial yoke, and the Marines were eager to avenge the Marine garrison overwhelmed there in the first week of war.

As the war grew more complex the code school in California expanded the code to a vocabulary of over 500 words, with specialized terms for new weapons, and many types of military activities not thought of by the developers. In addition, special terms were introduced for specific military objectives like islands and enemy bases.

The 2nd and 4th Marine Divisions would spearhead the original assault on Saipan. The senior officers of the 2nd Marine Division had never fully embraced the code program. That division's intense training schedule emphasized field skills and combat exercises, and as a result the talkers lost some of their skills through lack of use. Wilfred Billey was with the 2nd Marine Division. "We did send Navajo code talk, maybe as a message with high priority from Division headquarters. When I went on Saipan, John Benally and Roz Hosteen and it seems to me another person, they flew in from Hawaii. They tried to retrain us about the whole thing. And we reviewed some of the things."

On D-Day, June 15, 1944, Billy Chee landed with the 6th Marines. Their amtracs were driven north by a strong current, and concealed guns on Afetna Point emerged to rake the thin-skinned tractors. Billy watched in fascination as the tractor next to them simply disappeared in a cloud of black smoke, and a leg spiraled down to splash into the water. The tracks touched bottom, and with an audible crunch the tractor lurched forward and onto the beach. The rear ramp dropped, and Billy was propelled headlong outward by a violent shove from the company first sergeant.

Explosions formed a constant roar, interrupted by the snap of rounds passing close by and the metallic clank of rounds penetrating the tractor's side. As he rounded the rear corner of the tractor, a splash of gore hit him in the face, and he was knocked backward by the body of the man in front of him. Billy landed hard on his backside, but without missing a stride the first sergeant grabbed Billy by one belt suspender strap and heaved him up and forward.

The tractors had dumped the infantry under a series of ragged bluffs, and fire from caves and trenches was ripping into the Marines. NCOs and experienced men were already driving the others forward. The old NCO grabbed Billy by the belt. "Not you, Chief! Get on that thing and get us some naval gunfire."

Billy assembled the long antenna. Once he had a familiar task, he was filled with calm. This was a job he knew. "*Bil-dah-has-tanh-ya bi-tah-kiz tkoh tse-ye-chee.*" "We are pinned down between the water and the cliffs." Within minutes 5-in. shells from a destroyer were shrieking in.

On Saipan Wilfred Billey and many of the other code talkers were more often employed primarily as ordinary communicators, speaking in English. "Many times I had to go out with a company, and I would take the radio out, communications, voice, Headquarters Company would be commanding. I'd get this. Maybe not so much Navajo ..."

After dark on June 16 one of the sergeants told Billy to grab his gear and hurry up to B Company's positions. Listening posts had reported the sound

**BELOW LEFT**
PFC Cecil G. Trosip of the 4th Marine Division operates a generator clamped to a heavy chunk of Saipan coral. (NARA)

**BELOW**
On Saipan the improved Army SCR300 replaced the old TBY for front-line communications, though the TBY remained in use for ship-to-shore communications. Still called a "walky-talky," the radio had batteries with a much longer life. (NARA)

43

The SCR536 "spam can" or "handy-talky" radio, introduced on Saipan, provided lightweight, if sometimes unreliable, communications. In addition to stubby, rubber-coated short-range antenna, this one has the long-range antenna fitted. (NARA)

of engines and the distinctive sound of squealing tank tracks. Aerial observers had spotted two enemy tanks.

At 0330hrs next morning Billy heard a company request illumination, and a message requesting tank support. Fifteen minutes later a wave of Japanese tanks and infantry surged toward the Marine front. Artillery fire began to fall on the American artillery positions.

By 0415hrs the tanks had penetrated deep into the Marine positions. The glare from flaming tanks blinded the Marines to the approach of more tanks behind. The hard-hit artillery was supporting the defenders as best they could. Billy desperately relayed calls for naval gunfire support, shouting "*Ul-chi-uh-nal-yah!*," "Closer, closer!" as the tanks rumbled in. One tank bore down on a heavy machine gun position. The stubborn gunners held their ground, hammering away at the frontal armor until their tracers were no longer bouncing off. At the last moment the machine gunners scrambled out of the tank's path, and it crushed the abandoned gun. The tank rolled a few more yards. Flames spewed from every opening, but it cruised serenely off into the night with its dead crew.

Firing gradually died down as bazooka teams stalked the last enemy tanks. The largest tank battle of the Pacific War had almost annihilated the Japanese 9th Tank Regiment and the 136th Infantry Regiment, but far more blood would be spilled as the Marines pursued the enemy.

By this time a few senior code talkers like Carl Gorman had been promoted, and were performing more general duties as artillery and naval gunfire observers or as general communicators instead of the code talking duties for which they had been trained. The fighting on the larger island involved long-range patrolling and even mechanized patrols on the limited road network. Gorman was on one such patrol when their supplies ran out:

So all we had was two days' C-rations, and we ran out of it, and we were way behind the lines there for several days running around. There was no food, no nothing. So we got together, like, "What shall we do? Do you know any plants that we could eat here or something like that?"

I said, "Well, the Navajos are good at making broth." I said "We make broth from anything. Let's take all our jockey straps off, and boil it, and then … Then we'll drink the soup."

**E**    **NAVAL GUNFIRE OBSERVERS AND USMC CODE TALKERS IN ACTION NEAR GARAPAN, SAIPAN, 1944**

This typical small team of observers and code talkers is coordinating heavy naval gunfire and air strikes onto the coastal town of Garapan, a center of Japanese resistance. The harsh terrain, lack of water, and baking heat inflicted nearly as many casualties as the Japanese did. The observer on the left wears older P1940 utilities, and the code talkers wear a mix of P1940 and P1942 utilities. They have discarded leggings and even shirts in the intense heat. Their hasty position is a simple hole dug into the cliff top, with chunks of rock stacked around the edges. One code talker records messages, in English, in a message blank book, as the other translates and transmits to other code talkers. It was not unusual for the Marines to discard the camouflage helmet cover, as these men have done.

PFCs Carl Gorman and Jack Nez observe the bombardment of Garapan on Saipan, June 1944. The tattoo on Nez's arm is unusual, and both men appear to be wearing khaki (light tan) dress shirts in the intense heat. (NARA)

The northward slog through the cave-ridden and forested coral and volcanic hills was even less amusing. The 2nd Division was assigned the task of fighting their way up and over the highest mountains on the island. Food, ammunition, and copious volumes of water that allowed the men to survive in the intense heat had to be brought forward over trails laboriously hacked through the underbrush. The terrain was too rough for jeeps, and the carrier of choice was an infantryman's legs. Engineers rigged aerial trams from steel cables to bypass cliffs and the wounded or dead had to be brought back out along the same tortured path, with up to six men required to haul a stretcher up and down the rocky slopes. Blind valleys and deep limestone pits were choked with tangled vegetation, and combat ranges were measured in yards.

Intense heat was made worse by a shortage of drinking water. Rainfall quickly drained away into the limestone bedrock, and the Japanese fought desperately to control the few reliable wells. Late in the campaign torrential rains replaced the savage heat, and with it hordes of giant frogs came out to breed in puddles. Like many Marines, Gorman was frightened one night when a large frog jumped onto his back. Despite his adrenaline-driven attempts to kill it with his Kabar, the frog survived the encounter.

Two regiments of the 2nd Division were pulled out of the line for a rest when the fighting front reached the point where the island narrowed, but the Army's hard-luck 27th Division was mauled by a Japanese counterattack. The depleted 6th Marines were put back into the line.

Like many Marines, Billy Chee was horrified by what he saw near the north cape of the island. Bombarded by propaganda about Marine atrocities, Japanese civilians committed suicide in large numbers. Others were murdered by soldiers to "save" them from the Americans. Billy watched helplessly as one woman had her two small children lie on their faces. She battered their skulls in with a rock, and then hurled herself off a cliff. It was a sight that would haunt Billy and his fellow Marines for years to come.

From left to right, Corporal Oscar B. Ilthma and PFCs Jack Nez and Carl Gorman on Saipan. Note the ubiquitous M1 carbines. (NARA)

# JAPANESE ATTEMPTS TO BREAK THE CODE

After enlisting in the Army in March 1941, Joe Kieyoomia (pronounced <u>Kee</u>-o-mee) arrived in the Philippines in November 1941. When he was captured on Bataan, the Japanese concluded that he was Nisei, Japanese-American, because of the pronunciation of his name. Shipped to Japan, he was given the "opportunity" to admit he was truly Japanese. Frustrated by his insistence that he was an Indian from Arizona, his interrogators brutalized and tortured him, breaking his ribs and arm. The camp doctor, a British POW, treated his injuries as best he could, given that his only medical supplies were aspirin and rags.

As American forces approached Japan, in early 1945 the chief interrogator seemed to become aware that the mysterious transmissions must be in some North American Native language.

The interrogators had Kieyoomia listen to tapes of the broadcasts. The language the men were speaking was indeed Navajo but to Kieyoomia it was outright gibberish, a completely random jumble of words. It was clearly some

PFCs George H. Kirk (L) and John V. Goodluck photographed in a rest area on Guam. The "Smoky Bear" campaign hat is an unusual possession. Navajo did not typically collect souvenirs like the Japanese canteen and pouch hanging at the left. The helmet has both entry and exit bullet holes, and the knapsack is stenciled "G. H. KIRK USMC," a common practice. (NARA)

sort of spoken word-substitution code, but he had no idea how it worked. The code within a code was so complex that even a native-born speaker of the language could not make sense of it. Because the code was complex and constantly changing, even the capture of an actual code talker would not have granted the Japanese any more than a temporary advantage.

The interrogators "encouraged" Kieyoomia with more beatings. The interrogators beat him, stripped him naked, and made him stand on the wet parade ground in subfreezing cold.

When the Japanese summoned him back for his next interrogation, his feet had frozen to the ground. When he was beaten and shoved back toward the building, strips of flesh tore away from the soles of his feet, and he left bloody tracks across the parade ground. The daily interrogations grew increasingly frequent and brutal, but the Japanese were determined to keep him alive, since he was their only captive Navajo. The radio messages lifted Kieyoomia's morale, since the enemy's frantic efforts indicated that the Americans must be approaching Japan.

After months of mistreatment, Kieyoomia was transferred to a prison camp at Matsishima, 60 miles south of Nagasaki, arriving there the day before that city was struck by an atomic bomb. There he spent the last days before the final collapse of Japan.

# EUROPEAN COMBAT – THE COMANCHE

Some weeks after Nolly Bird's dangerous training experience at Slapton Sands, he was among troops cooped up aboard assault ships, lashed by a rainstorm and bobbing in waves inside an English harbor. Before midnight the ship slipped away and moved out into the rough Channel. For the remainder of the night the men were sleepless and exhausted, and even the men who were not seasick were nauseous from the smell of vomit. Before dawn the boat hove to, and began to roll in even more sickening spirals.

Without warning the boat pitched as the crew turned the engines to maximum and headed toward the dim eastern horizon. In the predawn light the boat grated onto gravel, throwing the passengers forward. The ramp dropped and Nolly plunged into chest-deep water, plowing forward and trying to hold the heavy radio shoulder-high, not trusting the black plastic

**COMANCHE CODE TALKERS IN ACTION, 4TH SIGNAL COMPANY, 4TH DIVISION, US ARMY ON UTAH BEACH, D-DAY**

The Comanche language code was far simpler than the Navajo code, without the complex word substitutions. Still, it baffled German field intelligence services. On D-Day the first message from Utah Beach, transmitted in Comanche, was "Right beach, wrong place," indicating that the landing boats had gone badly off course in the confusion and bad weather. This Comanche code talker has stripped the heavy water-proof plastic and tape from his SCR-300 radio, and set up for business near the water's edge. He has mounted the short antenna on the radio, since communications were direct line-of-sight to ships just offshore. In addition to the radio, he wears a communications specialist's wire tool in its canvas pouch on his belt near the pistol holster. This all-purpose tool was used to cut, strip, and splice field telephone wires. The nearby officer still wears his gas mask bag strapped to his leg, and the inflatable assault life belt (also shown in Plate C). Both items were usually quickly discarded, though for some reason the troops seemed to keep the life belt even after discarding the gas mask. In the background medical personnel, and a stranded sailor wearing the bulky naval crewman's life jacket, work to revive a drowned soldier. Behind them other infantry move inland through gaps blown in the wire entanglement, the primary obstacle along this isolated stretch of beach.

Follow-on troops of the 4th Infantry Division cross the broad stretch of shingle at Utah Beach, Normandy. The first message from the beach was in Comanche. The man at the far left has a BAR wrapped in plastic; it was typical to have crew-served weapons and radios wrapped in clear or black plastic protective sheeting. (NARA)

and tape to keep out the seawater. On the beach explosions threw pebbles as extra shrapnel. Machine-gun rounds whipped overhead. A man to his right ran for the shelter of a steel obstacle, but his lower body disappeared in a flash of light and dirt-laden smoke. The man tried to raise his remaining trunk on his hands, but collapsed and lay mercifully still.

"Chief! Get the hell over here!" shouted an officer, recognizable by the stripe on his helmet. "Get that radio going!"

Shivering with cold and fright, Nolly knelt on the rain-damp pebbles and stripped the plastic away. Fumbling with his map, the officer emitted a stream of curses. Nolly pressed the handset to his ear, and heard "... *kununa, Meekununa. Tsaaku nunnuwee. Atahtu nunnuwee.*"

"Major! It's Larry Saupitty, General Roosevelt's operator. He says we made a good landing. But we landed at the wrong place."

The major swore, but it was too late. His men were moving through gaps in the wire barrier. They were here, and here their war would start.

The following days were a blur of fatigue. One hot day the headquarters platoon was moving along a cow path when Nolly felt a flaming pain in his buttocks, and was knocked sideways into a muddy ditch. He never even heard the sound of the sniper's inexpert shot.

Nolly regained consciousness lying on his face looking at cow manure, his trousers around his knees. "Chief, I always said you was an asshole," said the calm, reassuring voice of the medic. "But FIVE? I think you got a million dollar wound here, old son." The medic stabbed the morphine ampoule into his hip.

Bird spent months in an English hospital. One of the least popular features of the Army's replacement system was that returning men were sent to a Replacement Depot, the infamous "repple-depples," from which they might be sent to a strange unit. Nolly was fortunate. He found his way back to the 4th Division in the late spring of 1945, in the relative safety of headquarters.

# FINAL CATACLYSMS

## Daily life – reorganization

Following the Central Pacific campaigns the Marine Corps began preparations for the assaults on the last islands before Japan. The accommodation at training bases had not changed, but there was a noticable change in the standard of living. The fully mobilized industrial might of America now provided more and better food and supplies.

**FAR LEFT**
The replacement for the TBX in selected applications was the new SCR610, like this one with the 7th Marines on Peleliu. (NARA)

**LEFT**
On Peleliu snipers and mortars firing from high ground held by the Japanese made any exposure dangerous. This communicator with the 3rd Battalion, 5th Marines is following a typical practice, raising the SCR300 for better reception in the rough terrain, but sheltering out of sight. (NARA)

The Marines themselves had learned many hard lessons, and changes were made in equipment and organization. New weapons and equipment were incorporated into the Division structure. The artillery assets that the code talkers could summon were far more powerful. The old 75mm howitzers were being phased out in favor of 105mm weapons, and 155mm guns and howitzers were available as amphibious corps assets. Most significantly, the divisions were extensively reorganized.

The new SCR300 backpack radio replaced the TBY, and the TBX in most applications. The new SCR536 "spam can" AM radio entered widespread use in infantry formations, though its low power limited usefulness. The field telephone remained a fundamental communications tool, and the only real improvement was better and lighter wire, and improved carriers.

Communications networks were more comprehensive, integrating various units through enlarged Signal Centers. The Signal Centers were a nexus for multiple radio and telephone nets, with the capability of relaying messages between the various systems. A typical Signal Center might include one or more code talkers to transfer spoken Navajo between telephone and radio links.

When the Marines left their rest and training centers for the next assault, they did so aboard specially designed ships – the Landing Ship Dock (LSD) that transported tanks, Attack Personnel Transport (APA)

In addition to other duties, the code talkers sometimes functioned as runners carrying messages handwritten on standardized message blanks. This runner is leaving a forward observation post on Iwo Jima. Note the map boards, binocular cases, and other scattered gear. (NARA)

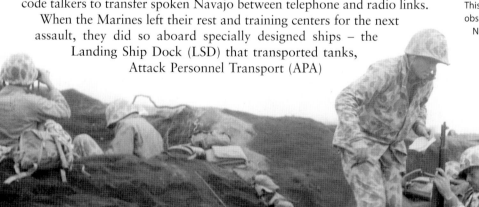

that carried troops, and the Attack Cargo Ship (AKA) for heavy equipment and supplies. Shipboard accommodation did not change much, since there was no perceived need to make Marines comfortable.

The increasing use of amtracs as beach assault vehicles prompted some of the biggest changes in the skills required of Marines. The LSTs were primarily mother ships to fleets of amtracs. The troops would be carried to the objective aboard APAs, and climb down the sides on rope cargo nets into waiting boats. Most would ride the boats to an LST, and climb up more nets onto the LST. Filing down into the vehicle deck, they would board amtracs, which would then drive down the LST's ramp and into the water for the assault.

The most comfortable duty for a code talker was undoubtedly aboard one of a new class of ships, the Amphibious Command Ship (AGC). These specialized ships served as a floating command center for division and amphibious corps commanders until facilities could be established ashore.

## The final battles

Peleliu, in the Palau Islands, was a controversial and bloody battle that perhaps never should have been fought. The Marines were assigned to capture Peleliu in fall 1944 to prevent air attacks from being launched against the rear of Douglas MacArthur's massive assault on the Philippines. Aircraft carrier raids revealed that the Japanese had no significant air capability in the islands, and Admiral William Halsey recommended cancellation of the invasion. Unable to communicate with MacArthur, who was under a radio blackout with his invasion fleet, the US Navy launched the attack anyway.

For the men of the 1st Marine Division Peleliu was a bloody, prolonged Calvary. Poor reconnaissance misidentified the jagged limestone hills as rolling terrain covered by trees, and the heat was almost beyond comprehension. Water supplies were polluted, and heat casualties were severe.

For the code talkers, it was the first battle where a map grid coordinate system, based on aerial photos, was used. It allowed even more security, as the coordinates would seem to the enemy to be a seemingly random jumble of words. For example, the cluster of buildings at the northern side of the main airfield, the staging site of a major enemy armored counterattack, was at map coordinate grid squares 129, A, B and C. "*Beh-bih-ke-as-chinigih Tlo-chin A-chin Ah-jah Dzeh Awoh Glo-ih A-kha sah Dzeh Tkin A-chin Ah-jah / Da-a'hl-Zhin / Be-la-sana Tsa-na-dahl Toish-je Tsa-na-dahl Tla-gin.*" What is written (number) Onion Nose Ear (ONE) Tooth Weasel Oil (TWO) Needle Ice Nose Ear (NINE) / period / Apple Tail Drop Barrel Tail Drop Coal (A, B, C).

For Operation *Detachment*, the assault on Iwo Jima in February and March 1945, the assault divisions would be the veteran 4th Marine Division and the inexperienced 5th Marine Division. The 3rd Marine Division would be the operational reserve, landing later. The initial waves would land in LVTs, with following waves in wooden LCVPs.

As in most divisions, endless days spent in field exercises caused code talkers to lose skills. In the 5th Division the Recon Company Commanding Officer finally intervened, pulling some of his men out of the relentless cycle.

Radios never replaced field phones, and most units had to coordinate the use of both, integrating the two nets at message exchanges like this one on Iwo Jima. (NARA)

One of the tasks of the Recon Companies was to help analyze beach conditions. They went toward the Iwo beaches on D-3. Because of rough surf the actual reconnaissance was left to skilled Navy swimmers, with the code talkers relaying messages from rubber boats offshore.

Vernon Begay had been assigned to the 25th Marines, 4th Marine Division. Two battalions, with one following, would land at the extreme north end of the landing beaches, just below a rock quarry. The rough waves off the exposed shore of Iwo, and the time spent in the tractors, assured that most of the Marines in Vern's amtrac would be exhausted and thoroughly sick long before they arrived on the beach. The LVTs wallowed along in line astern, parallel to the beach, as the Marines gawked at the roiling mass of explosions. The leading waves of tractors were already headed into the maelstrom.

At a signal from the boat leading the column, each tractor turned hard right and headed for the beach. The NCOs and officers drove the men down below the sides of the LVT. After the long run in, the tractor wallowed up onto the black sand beach, and veered around a stranded amtrac that was belching flames. Vern popped his head up, and heard the screams from inside the burning vehicle before his sergeant clouted him on the head and pushed him back down.

The ramp dropped and the passengers tumbled out in a rush. Hundreds of Marines were trying to scramble up the steep beach terraces, knee deep in volcanic sand. The sergeant looked at a white wooden stake driven deep into the sand and screamed at his men to get off the beach as the Japanese unleashed their pre-planned hell.

Mortar and artillery rounds rained down on the milling mass of men and tractors. One round impacted near Vern, but drove deep into the soft sand before exploding. The sergeant waved from the relative safety of a crater, and Vern tried to run but tripped over something. To his horror he saw that his foot was entangled in a long strand of human intestine.

A few seconds after Vern tumbled into the hole, a runner rolled down the sand terrace, and pounded on the sergeant's helmet. "Captain's up top. There's a row of pillboxes in back of flat ground. We need tanks, quick." Just as quickly, he was gone again.

Shaking with shock and fright, Vern was already bringing the radio online. "Arizona, Arizona." He repeated the battalion's call sign, and received an acknowledgement. "*Hane pesodi.*" Priority message. "*Nakia bil-dah-has-tanh-ya.*" Mexican (company) is pinned down. "*Jo-kayed-goh Chay-da-gahi ba-ah-hot-gli, shil-loh.*" Request tank support, urgently. "*Tah-bahn Dootizh A-la'ih.*" Beach Blue One. "*Shil-loh!*" Urgent!

Frontline switchboards were typically set up in any semi-sheltered place on Iwo Jima. The square symbols indicate a unit of the 5th Marine Division. The objects on top of the switchboard are dry cell batteries. (NARA)

Two miles out to sea a landing ship carrying three tanks of the 4th Tank Battalion turned toward the beach. Vern Begay had already earned his combat pay.

On D-Day the Recon Company of the 5th Division went in with the third boat wave. The Japanese were now pouring rounds from every gun at the boats and beaches. Navajo communicator Paul Blatchford watched as boat after boat was hit. He tried to convince the boat's coxswain to zigzag, but was told that the crews had orders to head straight in. Capt Thomas told Blatchford to "... line these boys up and have them kneel down, and check their belts, see if it's loose, in case we go over they can get rid of their packs ..." while he talked to the coxswain. Thomas got on the walky-talky, and "... finally I guess they all got the word, all the coxswains got the word, and then we took off. I noticed, everybody was going like that [zigzag gesturing], and every time they'd move the shells hit and missed them. And that's how we got to shore."

The Marines remained pinned down until tanks could be brought in to push toward Suribachi. The next morning the captain summoned Blatchford to go with him to observe the ground near the end of the Motoyama Number One airfield. "Just the moment we got there, we knelt down, we were talking ... and we got a shot right between us." The round went through a captured Japanese book the captain was holding "And boy – we got off there right away ..."

New men came in to replace the inevitable casualties. Blatchford told one nervous replacement to stay in his tracks, and under no circumstances to pick up souvenirs. Soon they were driven down by machine gun fire. When they could move again "I made about three steps, and all at once behind me, 'Boom!'..."

Blatchford turned and "He'd got off my trail and picked up something, I guess it was that booby trap, and when I saw him he was going fifty feet [15.2m] up in the air, and when he came down he was just hamburger."

It is common for one particular combat incident to be burned into the mind, and this was the one for Blatchford. "You know, when I came back, it used to just hit my head all the time. I just couldn't get over it for a long time."

One night the Recon Company was dug in, and code talkers were relaying messages among all three Marine divisions, coordinating positions, logistics, and determining the general situation when the Japanese came on the circuit.

Radio operators on both sides inevitably learned a few common words of each other's language simply by listening in on messages, and the code talkers understood a bit of simple Japanese. Blatchford and others thought the enemy radio operators were saying *kukajo* - this way. "So we said '*Kukajo, kukajo, kukajo*,' and then boy they started shelling," firing on an empty position the company had planned to occupy. "I told one of the boys, 'Go answer back, say *Haiee, haiee*.' That means yes."

The peculiar game continued for some time, the Japanese talking excitedly. A Nisei interpreter with the Marines was amused by the exchange. The interpreter just laughed. "... he got a great kick out of it. He said 'They don't even know who you guys are.' "

One lieutenant constantly ordered the men to shave. The Navajo communicators resisted, citing a belief that if you shaved or pulled your hair in battle, you died. Blatchford intervened with the captain. The lieutenant was nearby. " 'Is that true?' he said. 'Tomorrow I'll shave, we'll find out.'"

"So he did shave that morning, and at 9 o'clock he got shot right square in the forehead." Blatchford was told to pass the word that shaving was optional.

"After that, when they didn't shave anymore, why none of our outfit got killed again. And when it was all over, you know, a lot of these guys said 'By golly, you guys have a good religion.' "

Operation *Iceberg*, the invasion of Okinawa (March–June 1945), would prove to be the final battle of the war. The various Marine divisions continued their practice of utilizing – or not utilizing – the code talkers. Carl Gorman was serving as a communications specialist in the 2nd Marine Division, which conducted landings on the small islands around Okinawa. When the 1st and 6th Marine Divisions became badly depleted in the long and brutal campaign, one of the 2nd Division's regiments, and its supporting company of tanks, participated in the assault on the final Japanese stronghold at the extreme southern end of the island. The other two divisions used the code talkers in their intended role, transmitting high-priority messages.

Until the bitter end the code talkers taunted the clueless Japanese. Alex Williams Jr said that on Okinawa "... every time we'd try to send a message, they asked us in English, 'Who's this? We know it's Japanese talking.' Some boys would say 'Aw, the hell with you, Tojo. Get off.' " The Japanese were never very sophisticated at communications, and would retaliate by beating metal pans.

Carl Gorman, one of the Original 29, had participated in some of the bloodiest campaigns of the war, with no ill effects other than a case of malaria that laid him low about every six weeks. His luck finally ran out. While acting as a stretcher bearer, he was badly concussed by a nearby artillery explosion. Unable to shake off the combined effects of the explosion and the recurrent malaria, he was evacuated to a hospital on the west coast of the US. He was still there when the war ended.

Although a darling of photographers and film directors, the "spam can" radio was not particularly popular. The rough terrain and iron-rich rocks and soil of Iwo Jima severely limited its useful range, even with the long antenna. (NARA)

# AFTERMATH

All six Marine Divisions were in training for Operation *Olympic*, the first phase of the invasion of Japan, when the surrender came. Some men were retained for occupation duty in Japan and China, but most were discharged over a period of months. A senior communications officer gathered Vern Begay and others for a clandestine discussion. The Marine Corps still considered the code talker program a secret of the highest classification, and under no circumstances were they ever to discuss what they had done with anyone, including other Marines. The officer explained that the United States might soon find itself at war with the Soviet Union, and the code would again be invaluable. For the Navajo, their culture virtually forbade anything that might remotely suggest boasting. The communicators had simply done their duty. Most were like Carl Gorman, still recuperating in a hospital at war's end. He was given large bottles of quinine and atabrine for his malaria, and a ticket home.

Even after the Japanese surrender former POW Joe Kieyoomia continued to suffer from misconceptions about his ancestry. "... Red Cross officials thought I was from Singapore. I told them I was an *American* Indian."

Paul Blatchford was assigned to an intelligence unit in occupied Japan, transmitting secret reports. "... we had to transmit all the documents that the Army and the Navy wrote down, we transmitted at night, midnight, in Navajo, back to San Francisco, because they didn't want anybody to hear this." At Nagasaki, Blatchford observed "... Japanese with burnt arms and face, and they were just wrapped up with newspaper, you know. I guess that black ink got onto the sores and all that. They were just dying every day, and we had to report that too ..."

As a senior man, he was put in charge of a group overseeing Japanese POW demobilization. When some of the men needed to go to the head at a rail station, they asked Blatchford to help. He temporarily forgot the Japanese word, and decided to find an English speaker. Finally "... this fellow came up to me and said, 'Good morning'. So I said 'Good morning. Say, where's your head?' "

The Japanese was baffled by the Marine jargon. "He looked at me and said 'Oh, you sick in the head?'

"I said 'Oh, no, in the Marine Corps we say head. I mean toilet. Where is the toilet?'

" 'Huh?'

" 'I said toilet.' He didn't know." The Japanese shook his head and wandered off. By now the young Marines were increasingly agitated. Blatchford continued

**G**  **USMC CODE TALKER WEAPONS AND EQUIPMENT, LATE WAR PERIOD**

Over the course of the war the Marines adopted more modern Army weapons and communications equipment. The M1 Garand rifle (**1**) became the standard infantry squad weapon, and the M1 Carbine (**2**) replaced the Reising gun as the standard weapon for communicators. The Riot Gun (**3**), a militarized pump shotgun, was issued to security and communications units, and was a very popular and deadly short-range weapon. The hand-cranked generator (**4**) could be attached to a tree or pole with a chain clamp to provide power for a variety of radios. The lightweight SCR536 "Handy-talky" or "Spam™ Can" radio (**5**) with dry cell batteries at left, is often mistakenly referred to in postwar literature as the "Walky-talky." It had a very short range, particularly in rough terrain, and was not very popular with its users. The Navy EE8 remained the standard sound-powered field telephone throughout the war. Early versions had a leather carrying case (**6**), later replaced by a less expensive cloth carrying case (**7**). These field telephones were linked together at company and battalion level through portable field switchboards like those depicted (**8**). Connections were established by plugging connector cords, like those shown (**9**), into sockets. The Army Signal Corps SCR300 radio shown (**10**) was adopted by the Marines
but never fully replaced the TBX and TBY radios. The upper example shows the radio in use with the top open, and handset, earphones, and short range antenna fitted. The long, segmented AN-130-A antenna (**11**) allowed longer range; it could be disassembled and carried in a canvas bag. The lower illustration (**12**) shows the radio in its closed and sealed configuration, and the short-range antenna. The radio was powered by batteries like the BA-70 (**13**), carried in the box below the main radio unit.

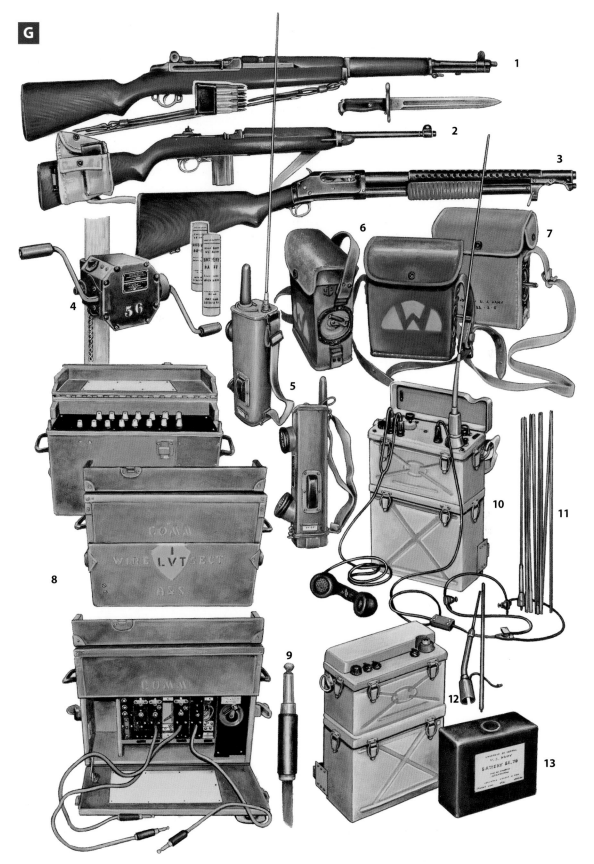

Private Jimmie Benallie (the name may be misspelled in the original caption), a code talker in the 1st Marine Division, stands outside a wrecked bicycle shop on Okinawa. (NARA)

to rack his brain. As the last Japanese approached "…. It just hit my mind, it was *benjo* – yeah – then I went up to him, and he said 'Oh, come on, right over there.'

"And then we went in there, you know, over there it's men and women all together. So we went in there and these guys said 'Chief, you took us in the wrong place.' "

The Army was more open than the Marines about their code talker program, but, in the joyous rush to demobilize, everyone just seemed to want to forget about it. Nolly and his Comanche comrades, like most veterans, just went home.

When Begay was discharged in early 1946, he noticed that the space for his Military Occupational Specialty was blank. The puzzled clerk was told by a sober-faced personnel officer to leave the space blank and to ask no more questions. There would be no record that Vern Begay was ever an MOS642, Code Talker.

The psychological effects of the men's experiences were less easily held secret. Paul Blatchford had been forever cured of any fear of the dead. After the war he conducted numerous burials in his community. Some, like Dean Wilson, who stayed in the Corps and was sent to northern China on occupation duty, were helped years later by community dances held for the most troubled. The possessions of the dead are particularly troublesome. "A lot of these souvenirs that they brought back, all of these had to be gone through by medicine men, yes. Otherwise, they had that – some effects from it, as long as you hang onto them."

Healing ceremonies could be as simple as the Blessing Way described by Alex Williams Jr. "Well, mostly good luck prayers, and our medicine men sing songs. You know, they have songs which they know only themselves. You have to pay so much to them, and then he'll take care of it with a lot of prayers and all. You know, quite a few, during that night, and usually two nights it lasts. The prayers will be mostly the first night, then the second, the next day it will be kind of quiet, and they give you a bath out of yucca leaves, and dry you then (with) the ground up corn, see, they usually dry you up with that, corn pollen, they use. You put clean clothes on, and you get the necklaces, belts, bracelets, and so on, that the Navajos wear. The final night, the last night, all the parents and relatives and all, they come in and be there too if you want them to come, and then of course the medicine man will be doing his heart's worth, with prayers and then singing all night. Finally it will be all night. They call it a good will thing ..."

Vernon Begay was wracked by nightmares, and would awaken his family screaming in his sleep. When he began to sleep with a knife in his hand, Manuelita Begay knew something had to be done. At some sacrifice, his family arranged a *Nidaa'*, an Enemy Way ceremony.

Vern waited weeks until the fortuitous months of summer, and the construction of the three prescribed temporary buildings; a temporary *hogan*, or house, for Vern, a small brush arbor for Manuelita and the children, and a combination cook shed and receiving room. On a Monday night, Vern sat in the *hogan* while friends, relatives, and neighbors visited to contribute gifts, and to eat mutton stew, fry bread, and coffee. Singers stood outside the *hogan*, and sang the sacred songs.

At dawn Vern's spokesman rode on horseback to the home of an old man who had known Vern as a child, and asked him to receive the ceremonial staff that would be prepared. The old man nodded gravely, and indicated the staff would be received on Friday. The ceremony always takes place over an odd number of days.

The following days were filled with a series of rituals designed to transfer the colorfully decorated juniper ceremonial staff to the staff receiver. Vern himself rode to the elder's home carrying the decorated staff, and presented it to a young assistant, who pronounced it good. The family of the staff receiver hosted another ceremonial meal for Vern's family. That night a large round-dance was held.

The old TBX radio soldiered on until the end of the war, like this one on Iwo Jima. (NARA)

On Friday the elder moved to the vicinity of the ceremonial camp, setting up a temporary camp nearby. After a breakfast served by Vern's extended family, the members of the elder's family sang more sacred songs outside the *hogan*, and received ceremonial gifts. While the healer sang and performed a ceremony inside the temporary *hogan* with Vern, Manuelita sat under the brush arbor, a shade created by four poles topped with vegetation, attired in special clothing that would be presented to her family from Vern.

That night the ceremonial participants, and anyone else who wished to attend, took part in more round-dancing as the high point of the ceremony. On Saturday morning everyone was exhausted as the healer and his assistants sang the closing songs of the ceremony. Whether it was through the intervention of the Old Ones, or simply practical psychology, Vern could live out his life in peace.

Like most veterans, the code talkers went quietly back into their communities. Like their white comrades, many became victims of alcoholism, but the vast majority went on to live productive lives. Their time off the reservations, and the educational benefits of the GI Bill, opened a new world. Many became educators, including Sam Billison, who earned a doctoral degree in education. Carl Gorman became a noted artist and instructor at The University of California at Davis, and Dean Wilson a tribal judge.

The Navajo code remained an ill-kept secret until former Marine Lee Cannon unwittingly set into motion the declassification of the program in 1969, by seeking to honor the code talkers at a division reunion. Only slowly did public knowledge of the secret communicators filter out until the code talkers were honored by a 1982 presidential decree. Because of the extreme secrecy, no one knows how many Navajo served as code talkers, or even who they were. Some have simply disappeared from history.

The role of the Comanche code talkers remains shrouded, not in secrecy, but in neglect. Charles Chibitty, the last Comanche code talker, died in July 2005. The role of the Army code talkers also remains one of the least-known aspects of the history of World War II.

The standard Japanese field telephone, though crude in construction, was compatible with US models. Unreliable communications and poor signal security were the bane of Japanese operations. (NARA)

# MUSEUMS AND COLLECTIONS

A number of local museums sponsored temporary commemorative displays during the period when the code talkers were receiving maximum publicity. Most were simply collections of photographs and text. The great majority of these displays have since been dismantled, but the following is a list up to date as of 2007. The traveler should be cautious, as small museums may close down without warning.

The small Navajo Code Talker™ Museum in Gallup, New Mexico, is located on historic Route 66.

Navajo Code Talker™ Museum, Tuba City, Arizona, is co-located with a hotel and tourism shop, the Tuba City Trading Post.

The Code Talkers Exhibit, National Security Agency Crypotologic Museum, Fort George Meade, Maryland, near Washington DC, is a small exhibit in a larger museum devoted to intelligence and strategic reconnaissance. From both a technical and historical standpoint it is perhaps the most significant. The exhibit includes TBY radios and other equipment used by code talkers.

The Burger King restaurant on Highway SR160 in Kayenta, Arizona, has a good privately owned display of artifacts including weapons, clothing, memorabilia, and period documents. The owner is the son of code talker PFC King Mike, who served on Okinawa. A permanent facility in a separate building is planned.

The Smithsonian Institution and The National Museum of the American Indian jointly sponsor two traveling code talker exhibits that will tour through 2011. A schedule can be obtained at www.sites.si.edu

The Choctaw Nation Capitol Museum in Tuskahoma, Oklahoma, maintains a small memorial display.

Establishing wire networks was still a dangerous and unwelcome task, as illustrated by this wire party in the jungles of Bougainville. (NARA)

# GLOSSARY

**amtrac**     any of several models of an amphibian tractor, a tracked landing vehicle, officially called an LVT (Landing Vehicle, Tracked).

**APC tablet**     a small white pill with aspirin and caffeine; it was considered the universal remedy for anything that ailed a Marine.

**AWOL**     Absent Without Leave. Being absent from a duty post, but with no evidence of intent never to return (desertion).

**boot camp**     the initial phase of Marine Corps training. Until his graduation, the recruit is not granted the title of Marine. He is constantly reminded that he is the lowest, dirtiest, smelliest piece of military equipment, or "boot."

**brush arbor**     four poles supporting a woven mass of cut vegetation, it provides shade in the desert.

**cadre**     several meanings. The relevant one is a group of veteran troops used to form the "skeleton" of a new unit. They provide experience and help train the newer men.

**code talker**     strictly speaking, the term refers to someone who communicates by voice using a devised spoken code. Someone simply speaking in another language is not a code talker. The reader should be aware that "Navajo Code Talker™" is copyrighted.

**coxswain**     the Navy or Coast Guard pilot of a small landing boat.

**DI**     a Drill Instructor, an experienced and proficient non-commissioned officer assigned to special training duty.

***Dineh* or *Dinee***     pronounced "Dee-Nay" "The People," the name the Navajo call themselves.

**dog-face**     Marine term for an Army soldier.

**E-boat**     large, high-speed, sea-going torpedo boat of the German Navy.

**glottal stop**     a slight pause or stoppage of breath, often very hard to hear, indicated by the symbol (') in linguistics. With the addition of a glottal stop, the Navajo word *tsin* (tree) becomes *tsin'* (bone).

**head**     Marine term for a toilet or latrine.

***hogan***     a Navajo house. Originally dome-shaped, built of wood and adobe mud.

**kabar**     generic Marine term for a heavy fighting knife, derived from the name of a manufacturer.

**LCP**     Landing Craft, Personnel. The first version of the Higgins landing boat, it had no bow ramp. Personnel climbed over the sides to disembark.

**LST**     Landing Ship, Tank. Vessel for landing heavy equipment. Paradoxically, they were sufficiently valuable as heavy transports that they were seldom used to land tanks in assault operations. Affectionately known to their crews and passengers as Large Slow Targets.

**MP**     Military Police. In a Marine Division one of their primary tasks is traffic control near the beachhead.

**Navajo**     a name coined by early Spanish explorers. Unlike some tribes, the *Dineh* do not object to this non-Native name applied to them.

**phase line**     Generally prominent linear map features, like streams or ridge lines, where rapidly advancing units would pause while units that were encountering more resistance could catch up. They prevented the development of open flanks, and helped minimize the chance of units calling down artillery fire on friendly units operating in front of them.

**pogey bait**     Marine term for candy or sweets.

| | |
|---|---|
| radio check | a test transmission to determine whether a link can be established. |
| round-dance | any dance in which the dancers rotate in a circle around a central point. |
| Shackle code | a simple alpha-numeric substitution code; it substituted groups of numbers for each letter in a message. Vulnerable to statistical code-breaking techniques, it was quickly compromised by the Japanese. |
| tonal language | a language in which the meaning of a word changes with the pitch going up or down, usually at the end of a word. To the English speaker they often have a sing-song quality. Vietnamese and "Valley girl" are familiar tonal languages. In Navajo *bini'i* can mean mind, nostrils, face, or waist, depending on intonation. |
| utility uniform | a heavy cotton uniform originally designed for day labor; it became the combat uniform for Marines. |
| *yata'ali'i* | a spiritual healer, or a specialist in conducting certain ceremonies. The terms shaman, medicine man, or singer are common translations, though none is truly descriptive. |

This captioned photo presented one of several wartime security breaches. It shows PFCs Edmond John, Wilsie Bitsie, and Eugene R. Crawford at the base camp on Noumea where veterans of the 1st Raider Battalion were sent to recuperate after the New Georgia Campaign. (NARA)

# REFERENCES

There are numerous publications on the code talkers, most produced as the result of publicity accompanying the declassification and recognition of the program. Most are quite superficial. The most highly recommended books are:

Durrett, Deanne, *Unsung Heroes of World War II, The Story of the Navajo Code Talkers: Facts on File*, New York, NY (1998). A children's level book, but quite useful

McClain, Sally, *Navajo Weapon: Rio Nuevo Publishing*, Tucson, AZ (1994)

Meadows, William C., *The Comanche Code Talkers of World War II*, University of Texas Press, Austin, TX (2002)

Other materials recommended for more in-depth research are:

Anonymous, *Last Meskwaki Code Talker Remembers*, Associated Press wire (2002). Can be viewed online at <http://www.usatoday.com/news/nation/2002/07/06/codetalkers.htm>

Doris Duke Indian Oral History Project, *They Talked Navajo – Dine Bizaad Choziid*, Navajo Tribal Museum, Window Rock, AZ (1971)

Frank, Benis M., *Oral History Transcript, Marine Corps Navajo Code Talkers*, History and Museums Division, Headquarters US Marine Corps, Washington, DC (1976)

Marcello, Ronald E., Interview With Carl Gorman, October 9, 1994, University of North Texas Oral History Collection, Number 1048 (1994)

Overviews with lesser research value include:

Jones, Catherine, *Navajo Code Talkers, Native American Heroes*, Tudor Publishers, Greensboro, NC (1997)

# INDEX